W9-BNA-072

SprinkleBakes

SprinkleBakes

Dessert Recipes to Inspire Your Inner Artist

HEATHER BAIRD

Author of the Award-Winning *SprinkleBakes* Blog

STERLING EPICURE
New York

STERLING EPICURE
New York

An Imprint of Sterling Publishing
387 Park Avenue South
New York, NY 10016

STERLING EPICURE is a trademark of Sterling Publishing Co., Inc.
The distinctive Sterling logo is a registered trademark of Sterling Publishing Co., Inc.

© 2012 by Heather Baird
Photographs © 2012 by Heather Baird

Designed by Christine Heun
Illustrations by Rebecca Schmidt Ruebensaal of Mr. Boddington's Studio

All rights reserved. No part of this publication may be reproduced,
stored in a retrieval system, or transmitted, in any form
or by any means, electronic, mechanical, photocopying, recording,
or otherwise, without prior written permission from the publisher.

ISBN 978-1-4027-8636-5 (paperback)
ISBN 978-1-4027-9166-6 (ebook)

Library of Congress Cataloging-in-Publication Data
Baird, Heather, 1975-
  Sprinklebakes : dessert recipes to inspire your inner artist / Heather Baird.
      p. cm.
  ISBN 978-1-4027-8636-5
  1. Cake decorating. 2. Icings, Cake. 3. Cookies. 4. Cake. 5. Desserts. 6.
Confectionery. 7. Cookbooks. I. Title. II. Title: Sprinkle bakes.
  TX771.2.B35 2012
  641.86'539--dc23

                              2011033141

Distributed in Canada by Sterling Publishing
c/o Canadian Manda Group, 165 Dufferin Street
Toronto, Ontario, Canada M6K 3H6
Distributed in the United Kingdom by GMC Distribution Services
Castle Place, 166 High Street, Lewes, East Sussex, England BN7 1XU
Distributed in Australia by Capricorn Link (Australia) Pty. Ltd.
P.O. Box 704, Windsor, NSW 2756, Australia

For information about custom editions, special sales, and
premium and corporate purchases, please contact Sterling Special Sales
at 800-805-5489 or specialsales@sterlingpublishing.com.

Manufactured in China

2 4 6 8 10 9 7 5 3 1

www.sterlingpublishing.com

For Mom

CONTENTS

INTRODUCTION

When I started my blog *SprinkleBakes* in September 2009, I wasn't prepared for the overwhelming response I'd receive from the food-blogging community. I'd always loved to bake, and I thought I had come up with some pretty good recipes and confections, but I couldn't have known the blog would take me on a journey that would change my relationship with my own creativity. Or that it would lead to the creation of this book!

I'd recently married Mr. Right after a whirlwind proposal and engagement, and we'd moved three hours outside of my native Knoxville, Tennessee. Now, three hours isn't a lot, but it meant that I couldn't commute to my beloved art gallery, which represents local artists of all stripes and is a place that inspires creativity and community. The atmosphere at the gallery had given my painting a real kickstart, and I had begun showing my own paintings there.

Now that I had moved away, it was goodbye, gallery; hello, new life! Instead of canvas, I was busy painting the walls of my new home. In the months to come, my hands were busy, and I still painted pictures occasionally, but I was still feeling the creative tug. My artwork was no longer being seen, which was not as satisfying. To me, an artist creates work to be enjoyed, but my paintings were propped up against the wall in a spare bedroom.

I began baking in earnest, and rediscovered the southern cuisine of my childhood. It was very much a creative release for me. As I experimented with flavors and

"Mr. Right!"

Biscuit

colors in desserts, the things I'd learned studying art came back to me. This was the beginning of my journey to artful baking.

I was being inspired by things I'd never considered. My creative impulses, which I feared had dried up, bubbled to the surface in exciting new ways. I found myself taking time to examine my surroundings. I was influenced by the seasons. The coziness of Christmas had my kitchen table filled with jars of port-wine jelly and gingerbread. Spring inspired tiny pink ruffled petit fours. I was further inspired by simple objects. A trip to the antiques store had me baking up vintage-inspired teapot cookies. Everywhere I looked I found inspiration. I had somehow managed to remove the creative blinders we sometimes wear while rushing around in our busy day-to-day lives. I began to focus on the beautiful things in life, and whatever inspiration I found I would take to the kitchen and re-create in my baking.

A friend once said to me, "Beauty hides in plain sight," and this rang truer than ever.

The deeper I got into cakes, cookies, and other desserts, the more apparent the similarities of baking and painting became. As a painter, I was most comfortable working in the abstract images of Cubism. The images and colors in a Picasso painting or sculpture may seem jumbled, but they are actually quite orderly. A face, structure, or object is taken apart and reimagined from an abstract and sometimes unnatural-looking perspective. Baking and pastry are very much the same. From the structure and order of recipes, I found ways to create delicious desserts with a new perspective, pleasing every one of my senses. They looked and tasted great, and, more important, made me feel something.

I love taking everyday objects or living things and reimagining them as beautiful, delicious desserts. It's even more exciting for me to take classic desserts and turn them on their heads, re-creating them as something even more fascinating to look at and to eat. Who says red velvet cake needs to be red? And why not think of another way to present a Yule log at Christmastime than just a stump from the woods? My training as an artist gave me a new sandbox to play in as a dessert maker, and I haven't looked back.

In this book, novice bakers will find foolproof recipes with easy-to-follow instructions. Experienced bakers will learn how to use their skills to tap into their creative process, how to think like an artist: begin with the structure and rules of good baking as your empty canvas, then let your imagination take you on a journey. My goal is to show you how to bake so that your dessert becomes the reward of your own creative endeavors and not the exact replica of a cake in a magazine or book. I will show you how a few simple lessons in drawing and painting, color theory, and sculpture can change the way you bake.

Just remember: every dessert is just a draft. If it winds up looking differently from what you had hoped, chances are it will still taste pretty good, so you can eat the evidence and try again. This book is about taking confection to the next level and giving it your own unique stamp. And having fun and eating well along the way!

In the words of Marshall McLuhan, "Art is whatever you can get away with." So why not start getting away with it in the kitchen?

one of my early paintings

GETTING STARTED

Every journey begins with a step, and in the dessert kitchen, that first step is having all your ingredients and equipment ready to hand. This section of the book contains a breakdown of my general rules of thumb when it comes to ingredients and techniques, as well as a detailed rundown of the equipment every artistically minded dessert maker should own. Refer back to this section for helpful information on making your SprinkleBakes-inspired creations!

BAKING EQUIPMENT

Using high-quality gear is essential when making dessert. Seasoned dessert chefs will have most of the cooking equipment listed here, but not necessarily all of the decorating equipment from the artist's toolbox. This is an alphabetical breakdown of most of the tools used in the book—if a recipe uses something that isn't on this list, it is usually mentioned at the beginning of the recipe.

Note: Choose sturdy aluminum baking sheets and pans, or better yet, a double-layer sheet (such as those made by AirBake), with a dull finish. These sheets will not warp or buckle as the oven temperature fluctuates, and they offer the most reliable results. Darker pans brown confections more quickly, so baking times may need to be reduced.

BOWLS: Graduated (or nesting) heatproof bowls are ideal for a variety of uses and are easy to store.

CANDY THERMOMETER: A candy thermometer is used for determining the various stages (soft ball to hard crack) of boiled candies. It is also used for tempering chocolate.

COOKIE CUTTERS: Cookie cutters come in an endless variety of shapes and sizes. Begin with graduated rounds and squares. Choose sturdy metal cutters. Tip: To prevent rusting, dry cookie cutters in the oven at a low temperature (120°F to 170°F) for a few minutes.

COOLING RACKS: Cooling racks allow air to circulate around the food. They are available in various sizes.

CUPCAKE/MUFFIN PAN (12-portion): These pans generally come in two muffin sizes, large and small. Beginning bakers need at least one such pan, but experienced bakers will want two (of each size!).

DOUGH CUTTER/SCRAPER: This flat metal tool is used to work with bread and pastry dough. It loosens dough from the work surface and is also used for cutting dough into pieces.

ELECTRIC HAND MIXER: An electric hand mixer is a convenient and portable alternative to the large stand mixer.

FLAT BAKING SHEET (no edges): An essential tool for bakers of every skill level; everyone should own at least two of these, and serious bakers will want more.

FOOD PROCESSOR: A food processor is useful for quick pie and tart crusts and is also handy for *sablée* or shortbread-type cookie dough.

GLASS BAKING DISH (13 x 9-inch): Everyone should have at least one of these, but dedicated bakers will want two. They are usually used for layered desserts and for cobblers and other fruit-based dishes.

JELLY ROLL PAN (11 x 14-inch, with low lip or edge): A useful pan for more than just jelly rolls, everyone should have at least one.

KNIVES: *Serrated knives* are essential for carving and leveling cakes, and *paring knives* can be helpful when trimming fondant or cutting out custom cookie shapes. And a 6-inch *chef's knife* for slicing and chopping is a must.

LIQUID MEASURING CUPS: These are available in 1-, 2-, 4-, and 8-cup capacities. The 4-cup is a good all-purpose size and suits most baking needs. Choose a heatproof-glass variety.

LOAF PAN (8 x 4-inch): Whether made of glass, ceramic, or metal, these have a variety of uses in the dessert kitchen. Everyone should have at least one.

MEASURING CUPS: A necessity for all baking projects, these come in graduated-size sets and are used for measuring dry ingredients or other foods that can be heaped into a cup, such as flour, sour cream, and vegetable shortening. I find stainless steel cups with pouring spouts the most useful and durable.

MEASURING SPOONS: Also a baking necessity, standard measuring spoons measure both wet and dry ingredients. My favorites are stainless spoons connected by a removable fastener.

OFFSET SPATULAS: These are helpful for loosening cakes from pans and are also useful for applying, spreading, and smoothing frosting on cakes. Purchase small, medium, and large offset spatulas with flexible blades.

PARCHMENT PAPER AND WAX PAPER: Parchment is used for lining cake pans and cookie sheets for flawless removal. It is needed for baking meringues and piping melted chocolate. Wax paper can also be used to line cake pans and is great for wrapping candies and caramels individually.

PIE PLATE (9-inch): Not just for pies any more! Every baker should have one, but seasoned bakers will want two.

PASTRY BRUSHES: Pastry brushes are used for buttering cake pans and glazing.

PASTRY RINGS: These are for molding individual desserts and can also be used as cookie or biscuit cutters. Four (3-inch-diameter) rings are a good set for beginners, but ambitious bakers will want six or even eight.

ROLLING PIN: This tool is essential for rolling out cookie dough and piecrusts. Choose a heavy wooden variety.

ROLLING-PIN GUIDE BANDS: These thick rubber bands slip on either end of a rolling pin to keep it at a precise distance from the dough, resulting in rolled dough that is perfectly uniform in thickness. This is especially desirable when preparing sugar cookies for decorating. Standard rolling-pin bands are usually sold in a variety pack of four sizes: 1/16-, 1/8-, 1/4-, and 3/8-inch thicknesses. Fondant rolling-pin guide bands are also available for rolling a precise thickness of gum paste and fondant.

ROUND PAN (9-inch): A must for anyone interested in making cakes, beginning bakers need two and daring bakers will want at least three.

RUBBER SPATULAS: These utensils are used for folding together whipped mixtures such as meringues, *macarons*, and sponge-based cakes. They are also used to efficiently scrape batters and icings from bowls and containers. Consider purchasing a variety of sizes, as they are very useful.

SIEVES AND SIFTERS: Comprised of a mesh bowl with a handle, sieves are used to separate unwanted solids from liquids and dry ingredients using a mesh screen. Sifters are a metal cylinder with a hand crank or squeeze handle. Sifters are used to aerate flour and other dry ingredients to create a light, fluffy texture in baked goods.

SPRINGFORM PAN (9-inch): An essential tool for making many different desserts, beginning bakers need one and experienced bakers three or more, depending on their ambitions.

SQUARE GLASS BAKING DISH (9 x 9 inch). Everyone needs one, but most bakers will want two.

STAND MIXERS: These are more powerful than hand mixers. Stand mixers have interchangeable attachments: a whisk to beat eggs and cream, a paddle attachment to mix thick dough, and a dough hook to knead yeast breads. These mixers make preparing wedding cakes and other large-quantity batters an easy task.

TART PAN (9-inch): Everyone needs at least one of these scallop-edged shallow pans.

WHISKS: Available in metal and silicone-coated varieties, whisks whip and aerate; they are used to blend ingredients quickly and efficiently. A large metal balloon whisk is ideal for beginners.

ART SUPPLIES
AND DECORATING TOOLS

Before embarking on a SprinkleBakes project (especially the ones in the Mixed Media chapter, beginning on page 228), make sure you have all the art supplies you need ahead of time. Some of the items I recommend here, such as scissors, pencils, and paper, are common household items you probably already have.

CAKE BOARDS: These are usually made of strong corrugated cardboard and come in a variety of shapes and sizes. Find them at cake supply stores in decorative colors and metallic coatings.

DISCO DUST: This edible glitter is used to decorate confections.

FONDANT CUTTERS: Much like plastic cookie cutters but smaller, these are available in a wide variety of shapes and sizes, including letters and numbers.

FONDANT ROLLERS: Fondant rollers are plastic rolling pins that have a nonstick surface and leave a smooth finish on rolled fondant. (Wooden rolling pins can leave unwanted wood-grain impressions.) Fondant rollers come in various sizes. Large cake projects will require a large fondant rolling pin.

FONDANT SCULPTING TOOLS: These small plastic tools are for shaping flowers and other decorative flourishes.

FONDANT SMOOTHER: Essential for shaping fondant around cakes, fondant smoothers press out air bubbles trapped under fondant for a smooth, even finish. Beginners interested in fondant application should purchase this inexpensive and useful tool.

FOOD COLORING: Used to tint batters and icings, food coloring is available in liquid, soft gel, gel, and ultraconcentrated powders.

FOOD WRITERS: Food writers are felt-tip markers filled with edible coloring.

HEAVYWEIGHT CRAFT PAPER OR POSTER BOARD: These can be used for making cutout templates.

LUSTER DUST: These pearlescent shimmering powders are available in various colors at craft and cake supply stores and are applied on smooth confectionery surfaces with an artist's brush. Be sure to purchase food-safe, edible luster dust.

NONPAREILS, DRAGÉES, SPRINKLES, AND QUINS: These small decorative pellets of sugar are used to decorate cakes, candies, and cookies.

PAINTBRUSHES: Used to apply color and embellishment to confections, paintbrushes can also be used to brush away fine crumbs and confectioners' sugar. If you are an artist or a crafter, keep a separate set of brushes in the kitchen and use them only for baking.

PENCILS: Retractable pencils are used to draw templates and sketch ideas. Keep one in your decorator toolbox.

PIPING BAGS: Available in cloth and disposable plastic, piping bags are a must when piping icings and intricate designs with decorative piping tips. Basic piping can be done in a pinch using zip-top bags (see adjacent).

PIPING TIP BRUSH: This small, two-in-one tool is used to remove blockages and hardened icing from piping tips.

PIPING TIPS AND COUPLERS: Piping tips are used for piping three-dimensional shapes such as flowers, stars, and decorative borders. Plastic couplers must be used to affix piping tips to piping bags and are essential for ease in switching tip sizes while decorating.

RULER: A ruler is used for template making and a variety of measuring tasks—use a plastic or stainless steel ruler that can be easily washed.

SCISSORS: Scissors are used to cut out templates and trim fondant pieces and gum paste. I recommend purchasing a pair solely for cooking purposes that can stand up to repeated cleaning.

TWEEZERS: Tweezers are useful when applying dragées or tiny decorative flourishes to cakes and confectionery. Keep a dedicated dessert tweezer in your baking toolbox.

X-ACTO KNIFE: X-Acto knives are used to cut fondant and gum paste and are useful in precise template cutting. As with the tweezers, this X-Acto knife should only be used for dessert-making!

ZIP-TOP PLASTIC BAG: These are handy for storing everything from nuts to paintbrushes, and in a pinch can be used as a substitute for a piping bag: After filling the bag with batter or icing and firmly closing the top, snip a corner and pipe when ready.

BAKING COMMANDMENTS

For any artist, there are standard rules to remember: have a plan; work with clean surfaces and equipment; immerse yourself in a work environment that is relaxing and distraction free. Baking is no different. Below are my "commandments"—rules I follow every time I walk into the kitchen and begin creating an edible piece of art.

TECHNIQUES

MISE EN PLACE: This French phrase means "everything in place," or simply, have all your ingredients prepared before you start baking. Doing a little prep work before you bake can greatly relieve stress when the time comes to put everything together. Measure ingredients ahead of time. Have fruit washed and patted dry. Chop chocolate and nuts. Make sure cooling racks are ready to receive hot pans. Thinking ahead is especially important when dealing with recipes with time constraints or lots of steps.

MEASURING: When using a large glass measure (2-, 4-, or 8-cup), place it on a flat work surface at eye level for an accurate measurement. Use liquid measuring cups for liquid and flat metal or plastic graduated-size cups for dry ingredients. Do not measure flour, sugar, or other dry ingredients in glass liquid measuring cups. It is impossible to level ingredients, causing amounts to be uneven, which affects the outcome of the recipe. Spoon flour into dry measuring cups until overflowing, then level the mixture with a long metal spatula or the back of a straight serrated knife. Finally, avoid scooping flour directly from the container; doing so can cause the flour to become compressed in the measuring cup, and baked goods will have a dense texture.

GREASING BAKING PANS: I almost always use white vegetable shortening to grease baking pans. It is clear and mostly tasteless. Unless specified in a recipe (such as that for *Financiers*, on page 38), I avoid using butter because it contains milk solids that can burn and contribute to overbrowning.

Oil sprays can be used for ease and convenience, but in my experience, they do not provide consistent results for clean cake removal. In place of oil sprays, I recommend flour-based baking sprays such as Wilton's Bake Easy or Nordic Ware's Baker's Joy. They are more expensive than regular oil sprays, but provide good, consistent results.

COMBINING INGREDIENTS: When using a stand mixer, stop the motor to scrape down the sides and bottom of the mixing bowl intermittently. Despite its many speeds, the stand mixer has but one mechanical movement. Because of this, pockets of wet and dry ingredients occasionally become trapped at the bottom of the bowl or flung high upon the sides of the bowl and out of the mixing attachment's reach.

FOLDING BATTER: Meringue, whipped eggs, and whipped cream are often combined with other ingredients to create a light texture in desserts. To avoid deflating whipped ingredients, use the folding technique to incorporate the mixture.

Use a large rubber spatula as your folding tool.

Place the ingredients into a bowl as directed by the recipe. Sometimes a recipe asks you to fold one-third of the whipped ingredient into the mixture to "loosen" it. Other times the entire amount is folded in at once.

Using the thin edge of the spatula, cut through the middle of the ingredients in a straight line. With a scooping motion, scrape the bottom of the bowl and turn the ingredients over with the spatula as you bring it to the surface. Turn the bowl counterclockwise (toward yourself) with your free hand as you do this.

Repeat until the batter is consistent and no streaks of whipped ingredients remain.

TESTING THE DONENESS OF CAKES: Check cakes 5 to 10 minutes before removing them from the oven. You can do this by inserting a toothpick into the center of the cake; if it comes out clean, the cake is ready to be removed from the oven. If wet batter clings to the toothpick, return the cake to the oven and recheck at 5-minute intervals. Alternately, gently press the center of the cake with a fingertip to check for doneness. If indentions are left in the cake, it needs to bake longer. If the cake springs back when the pressure is removed, it is done.

INGREDIENTS

BUTTER: Use the highest-quality butter possible whenever you bake. Unsalted butter is used unless otherwise noted. To soften a stick of butter, let it stand at room temperature for 15 to 25 minutes; check it at 15 minutes. If you're in a hurry, take a stick of butter directly from the refrigerator and place it unwrapped in a microwave-safe dish. Heat the butter in the microwave for 10 to 20 seconds. The butter should still be slightly cold and should hold an indention when a finger is pressed into its surface.

CANDY-FLAVORING OILS: Oils made for flavoring hard candies and chocolates are more potent than extracts. They are sold in small containers (often called "drams"), and because they are so potent, they can be added a drop at a time with a new (unused) eyedropper. Most extracts contain water and cannot be added to melted chocolate. Just a small amount of water in melted chocolate will make it seize (or become chunky, hard, and grainy) and render it unusable.

CHEMICAL LEAVENS: Baking soda, baking powder, and cream of tartar should all be checked for expiration dates before being used for baking. These leavens lose their potency over time, and using an old product can result in dense and poorly risen baked goods.

CITRUS ZESTS: Zests can be added to cake batters, cookie doughs, icings, fillings, even tart crusts. Use a fine grater (such as Microplane brand) for thin, wispy flakes of citrus zest. Wash and dry citrus thoroughly; grate the outermost layer of the fruit, as it holds all the color and flavor. Avoid using the white part of the peel, called the pith, which has a bitter taste.

COFFEE: Coffee can be used to flavor all types of confections. Instant coffee granules or espresso powder can be added to cookie dough, meringue, cake batter, and icing. Along with the instant varieties, strongly brewed coffee can be used in chocolate desserts to greatly enhance the flavor. Use coffee in chocolate mousse, chocolate cakes and tarts, chocolate truffles and icings . . . anytime your chocolate confection needs a flavor boost.

EGGS: Use grade A large eggs for the recipes in this book. USDA eggs of this grade and size are approximately 2 ounces each. Extra-large, jumbo, or farm-fresh eggs may be too large, and the excess moisture can cause batter to be lax. Be sure to note if a recipe requires eggs to be brought to room temperature before using. In general, eggs should be brought to room temperature before adding to cake batter to achieve maximum volume, prevent the butter from seizing (that is, re-solidifying), and create a smooth batter. It takes 15 to 20 minutes for eggs to reach room temperature, or they can be placed in hot (not boiling) water for 5 to 10 minutes.

EXTRACTS: Most extracts are made with natural botanic oils and have an alcohol base. They are often used by home bakers, as they are widely available at grocery stores. Use extracts in all forms of baked goods. Artificial flavorings are not recommended for the recipes in this book.

FLOUR: I use primarily bleached, all-purpose flour in my recipes. In keeping with my southern heritage, I use White Lily flour (as any other brand is frowned upon by the elders in my baking tribe). In my weaker moments I have been known to use unbleached flour, such as King Arthur's, and you can, too. Cake flour can be substituted for all-purpose in equal amounts for a lighter texture in cakes, but a lighter cake is not always desirable. For instance, cake flour is not recommended for tiered cakes or for cakes that are to be carved; all-purpose flour has more gluten and creates a much stronger structure.

HERBS AND SPICES: Most consider herbs for savory use only, but adding fresh herbs to sweets can add amazing nuances of flavor. Culinary lavender is delicious in shortbread and butter cake. Basil, lemon balm, and mint pair harmoniously with chocolate. Thyme is delicious with citrus fruits. Because fresh herbs are so potent, mince herbs finely before adding to batter or dough. Alternatively, fresh herbs may be steeped in milk or heavy cream to extract their flavor. Herb-infused milk can be used in cake batter, and herb-infused cream can be used in chocolate ganache. Apart from dried culinary lavender, dried herbs are not recommended for use in baked goods because of the bitterness they impart. Cinnamon, ginger, and nutmeg are all well-loved baking spices for good reason. Adding a teaspoon or two to baked goods creates delicious aroma and flavor. These days, savory spices are being unconventionally added to sweet confections. Cayenne pepper, smoky paprika, wasabi powder, and ground mustard are just a few that pastry chefs and chocolatiers are adding to their creations. Use a small sprinkling of ground spices to top chocolate truffles. Cayenne pepper can be used to spice up chocolate cake. Use ground mustard to punctuate the other spices used in spice cookies. Utilize daring spices in sweets judiciously—begin with small amounts. Make sure they are well distributed in batter and dough.

These spices can be overpowering, and biting into a large amount of spice can be unpleasant. Finding inspiration for spicy sweets is easy. Take notice of unconventional flavor pairings at your local bakery or when browsing specialty chocolate shops; try to replicate the flavors that pique your interest in your own baked goods. Soon you'll be fearlessly baking up your own flavor ideas.

LIQUEUR AND WINE: Liqueur can enhance the flavor of berries and fruit compotes. Pair fruit liqueurs with their fruit counterparts: soak fresh cherries in kirsch or blackberries in blackberry brandy before adding them to baked goods. Dried figs and raisins can be rehydrated by heating them in a saucepan with wine. Pears and other pale-flesh fruits turn a beautiful color when poached in red wine.

SUGAR: Standard granulated sugar can be used in most recipes, but when making meringues or whipped egg batters such as for *Genoise* Sponge Cake (see page 40), use superfine granulated sugar. Superfine sugar is ground finer than regular granulated sugar and will say so on the package; this is not confectioner's sugar, which is ground so fine that it has cornstarch added to it to prevent caking. Superfine sugar dissolves easily, so confections keep their lightness and height during baking. If you don't have superfine sugar or can't find it at your grocery, you can create your own by grinding standard granulated white sugar in a food processor for several minutes until fine and powdery.

BLANK
CANVASES

Much like a painter's blank canvas, these recipes
are ready to be decorated with art. Cookies,
cakes, and candies can be endlessly varied
with flavor, color, and shape. Use these trusty
recipes time and time again, whether it
is to create a confectionery work of art
or just to satisfy a craving.

COOKIES

THINGS TO KEEP IN MIND

▨ To allow cookies to brown evenly, use flat, heavy-duty baking sheets with a dull finish. These sturdy pans will not warp under heat.

▨ If a cookie recipe calls for the pan to be greased, use white vegetable shortening. Butter and margarine are not suitable for this task and will scorch pans. Most of the cookies in this book require the use of parchment paper to line the baking sheet.

▨ Cookie ingredients are often mixed together in the same way; butter and sugar are creamed together, then the liquids are added, and finally the dry ingredients are incorporated. All ingredients should be mixed until just combined. Overmixing can make cookies tough. Unless otherwise indicated, use a stand mixer fitted with the paddle attachment on low speed to combine dough. If you don't have a stand mixer, you can use an electric hand mixer on the slowest setting. And of course, you may also choose to mix cookie dough by hand with a wooden spoon, though this takes longer and is more labor-intensive.

▨ Bake same-size cookies on the same pan so they all will be finished baking at the same time. This is especially important when creating various shapes and sizes of cutout cookies.

▨ Cookies high in sugar and fat can brown quickly. Check cookies 5 minutes before the suggested time to avoid overbrowning.

SIMPLE SUGAR COOKIES

YIELD: Approximately 30 (3-inch) cookies

This sturdy and slightly sweet sugar cookie is my favorite for decorating. The dough contains no chemical leavening agent, so the cookies won't puff up or lose their shape while baking.

½ pound (2 sticks) butter, softened
1 cup plus 2 tablespoons granulated sugar
1 egg, lightly beaten
1 teaspoon vanilla extract
3 cups all-purpose flour, plus more for rolling
Pinch of salt

---

1. In a stand mixer fitted with the paddle attachment, mix the butter and sugar together until just incorporated. Do not over-mix at this stage, or the cookies may spread while baking.

2. Add the egg and vanilla extract. Mix again on low speed, stopping to scrape down the sides of the bowl intermittently as needed.

3. Add the flour and salt. Mix on low speed until a dough is formed and there are no longer any streaks of butter in the mixing bowl. The dough will often clump around the paddle attachment while being mixed. This is normal and a good sign that your dough is the right consistency.

4. Line a baking sheet with parchment paper.

5. Turn the dough out onto a sheet of plastic wrap and form into a ball. The dough will not be sticky and should be easy to work with your hands. Wrap the dough tightly and refrigerate for 1 hour.

6. Working on a well-floured surface, knead the dough slightly, squeezing it with your hands to flatten the ball into a disc.

7. With a floured rolling pin, roll dough to a ¼-inch thickness. For perfectly even dough, you may use guide bands or two flat ¼-inch dowels as guides on either side of your workspace.

8. Cut out desired shapes from the dough and transfer to the prepared baking sheet. Be careful not to stretch the cutout shapes or they will be distorted after baking.

9. Refrigerate the cutouts for 30 minutes. This will help the cookies maintain a crisp shape during baking.

10. Preheat the oven to 350°F.

11. Bake the cookies for 15 to 20 minutes, or until golden brown around the edges.

12. Let cool on the baking sheet for 5 minutes. Transfer to a wire rack. Decorate the cookies when completely cooled.

VARIATION

Chocolate Sugar Cookies: Measure 1 level cup cocoa powder. Remove 2 tablespoons cocoa and replace with 2 tablespoons flour. Use this to replace 1 cup of the flour in the recipe.

A. The dough will form clumps when it is properly mixed. **B.** Roll out the dough on a well-floured surface. **C.** Cut out the desired shapes.

SHORTBREAD

YIELD: 24 (3-inch) cookies

The key to making great shortbread is using the best-quality butter you can find. This recipe contains an entire pound of butter, and the end result is a slightly sweet, buttery-tasting, crumbly cookie that is perfect with coffee or tea.

This recipe can be flavored with citrus zests, extracts, spices, or chocolate chips. There are a great number of flavor possibilities, and if you are feeling adventurous, the addition of matcha green tea powder makes a colorful and flavorful cookie.

1 pound (4 sticks) butter, softened
¼ cup granulated sugar
1 cup confectioners' sugar
1 teaspoon vanilla extract
4 cups all-purpose flour, plus more for rolling
Pinch of salt

1. In a stand mixer fitted with the paddle attachment, beat the butter and granulated sugar until light and fluffy.

2. Add the confectioners' sugar and beat until incorporated.

3. Add the vanilla extract and mix again.

4. Add 2 cups of the flour and the pinch of salt and mix on low speed until a dough forms. Add the remaining 2 cups of flour and mix again on low speed until a very stiff dough forms.

5. Gather the dough together with your hands and place on a lightly floured surface. Divide into two pieces. Using a floured rolling pin, roll each piece of dough until flattened to about a 1-inch thickness.

6. Wrap the dough in plastic film and place the pieces on a cookie sheet or jelly roll pan. Refrigerate for 30 minutes. This dough will firm up quickly because of the high butter content.

7. Preheat the oven to 350°F. Line a cookie sheet with parchment paper.

8. While it's still cold, roll out the dough to a ¼-inch thickness. If the dough is difficult to roll, let it stand at room temperature for a few minutes until it is pliable. Use rolling-pin guide bands for evenly rolled shortbread.

9. Cut the dough into desired shapes. Place the shapes approximately 1½ inches apart, on the prepared cookie sheets and bake until lightly golden around the edges:

- 7 to 10 minutes for small cookies
- 12 to 15 minutes for medium cookies
- 17 to 20 minutes for large cookies

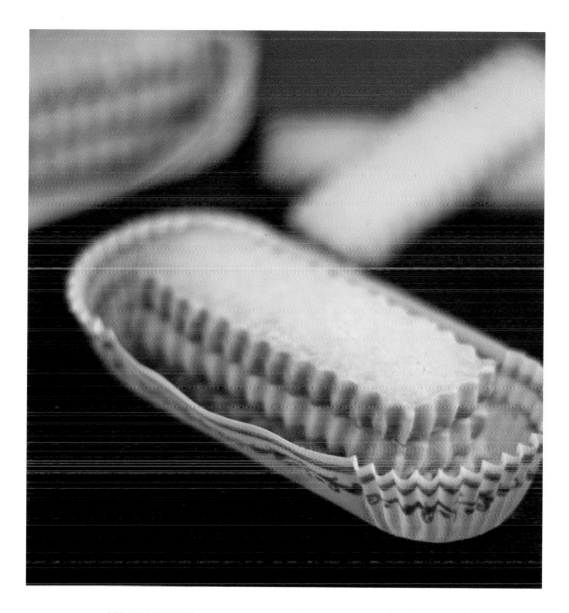

VARIATIONS

Chocolate Shortbread: Decrease flour by ½ cup and add ½ cup of Dutch process unsweetened cocoa powder.

Chocolate Chip Shortbread: With dough in stand mixer, pour in chocolate chips and mix on lowest speed until chips are evenly dispersed.

Cinnamon Spice Shortbread: Add 2 teaspoons cinnamon to the creamed butter and sugar.

Matcha Shortbread: Add 2 tablespoons matcha green tea powder to the creamed butter and sugar.

Orange or Lemon Shortbread: Add 2 tablespoons citrus zest to the creamed butter and sugar.

GINGERBREAD COOKIES

YIELD: 36 to 60 cookies or 1 large gingerbread house and accoutrements

If you need a dependable recipe for spicy, fragrant gingerbread dough, look no further. I love this recipe because it is soft enough to enjoy as a cookie and sturdy enough to create architectural pieces for gingerbread houses.

---

2 teaspoons baking powder
2 teaspoons ground ginger
1 teaspoon baking soda
1 teaspoon salt
½ teaspoon ground cinnamon
1 cup vegetable shortening, at room temperature

1 cup sugar
1 cup dark molasses
2 eggs, at room temperature
2 teaspoons white vinegar
5 cups all-purpose flour

---

1. In a small bowl, whisk together the baking powder, ginger, baking soda, salt, and cinnamon.

2. In the bowl of a stand mixer fitted with the paddle attachment, cream together the shortening and sugar, scraping down the bowl as needed.

3. Add the bowl of spices to the creamed sugar mixture; beat until just incorporated.

4. Add the molasses, eggs, and vinegar. Beat until the mixture is well combined. At this stage, the fat may separate a little and the batter may look curdled, but this is normal.

5. Beat in the flour 1 cup at a time. Begin on low speed and mix until the flour is just incorporated; increase to high speed in short bursts until well blended.

6. Turn the dough out onto a sheet of wax paper and press flat with your hands—the dough should not be sticky.

7. Top the dough with an additional sheet of wax paper and gently roll with a rolling pin to even the dough's surface. Wrap the dough—wax paper and all—in plastic wrap and chill thoroughly in the refrigerator before using, at least 3 to 4 hours. For best results, chill overnight.

8. Preheat the oven to 375°F. Line a baking sheet with parchment paper and set aside.

9. When the dough is firm, roll dough to desired thickness. For cookies, roll the dough to ⅛ inch thick; for gingerbread-house pieces, roll to ¼ inch thick. Cut the dough with cookie cutters or use a sharp plain-edge knife to cut around handmade templates.

10. Place cookies on the prepared baking sheet 2 inches apart and bake:

- 12 to 15 minutes for small, thin cookies
- 20 to 22 minutes, or until firm to the touch, for large cookies or gingerbread-house pieces

A. Well-mixed dough. **B.** Press the dough flat with your hands. **C.** Use rolling pin guide bands to roll the dough to an even thickness.

MERINGUE

YIELD: Approximately 36 cookies

Whip up a couple of egg whites with a little sugar, and magically you have meringue—sculptural, versatile, beautiful meringue.

Baked meringue has a high sugar content and is baked at a low temperature for a long period of time. It can be piped into mushrooms (for classic *bûche de Noël* décor), cookie kisses, or edible containers.

---

2 egg whites, at room temperature
Pinch of cream of tartar
½ cup superfine sugar

---

1.   Preheat the oven to 170°F. Line two cookie sheets with parchment paper. Fit a large pastry bag with desired tip. Use a large star tip for kisses or a plain or slightly fluted decorating tip for bowls or containers for fresh fruit, custard, lemon curd, or other fillings.

2.   Place the egg whites in a spotlessly clean bowl and whip them with an electric mixer on medium speed until frothy.

3.   Stop the mixer and add the cream of tartar. Start the mixer again and continue to beat the egg whites.

4.   Once the egg whites form soft peaks, increase the speed to high and gradually add the sugar, a little at a time.

5.   Beat the egg whites until they are very shiny and hold stiff peaks but are not dry or crumbly, about 7 minutes.

6.   To make sure the sugar has completely dissolved, rub a bit of the meringue between two fingers to see if any granules of sugar remain. If grains are present, continue to beat the meringue until the sugar has fully dissolved.

7.   Spoon the meringue into the pastry bag and pipe onto the prepared cookie sheets. Meringue can also be dolloped onto parchment by heaping spoonfuls if you have no piping bags or decorator tips.

8.   Bake the meringues for 90 minutes, turning them halfway through the cooking time to ensure even cooking.

9.   When the meringues are done, turn off the oven and let them stand in the closed oven for several hours or overnight. The meringues should be hard and dry to the touch, and you should be able to easily lift them from the parchment.

VARIATION

To create a Meringue Cup: First, pipe a 3-inch round spiral of meringue on a piece of parchment paper. Then pipe layers on top of the outer edge of the base, making three to four passes, spiraling upward to create a wall of meringue. Bake according to recipe instructions.

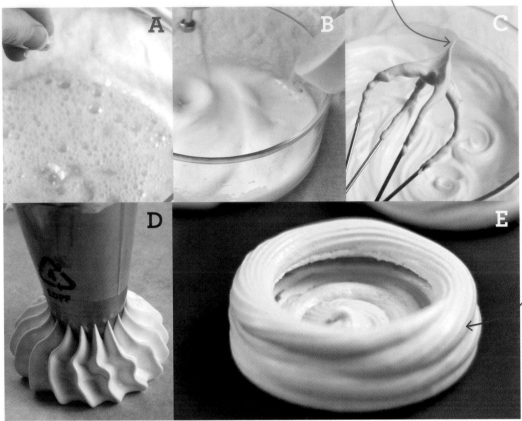

stiff peak!

fill this with pastry cream and berries

A. Sprinkle cream of tartar over the egg whites. **B.** Slowly pour in sugar as you beat the egg whites. **C.** Beat the egg whites until stiff peaks form. **D.** Pipe the meringue onto parchment using a fancy decorator tip. **E.** The meringue can be piped to form containers.

TIPS FOR MERINGUE SUCCESS

- Always make sure bowls and beaters are spotlessly clean. Any trace of grease or fat will keep the egg whites from whipping properly. For this reason, you should be very careful to not get egg yolk in your egg whites. Just a little drop can ruin the meringue.

- Superfine sugar dissolves more easily than regular granulated sugar and helps meringue maintain a light texture.

- Avoid making meringues during humid weather. Humidity causes meringues to collapse and become sticky.

- When making baked meringues, turn the oven off after the timer has ended and leave the meringues in the oven overnight. This way the meringues will cool slowly in the oven, making them less likely to crack.

LADYFINGERS

YIELD: Approximately 30 cookies

These delectable biscuits are known by several names—*savoiardi*, sponge fingers, and boudoirs, to name just a few—but I've always known them as ladyfingers. They are perhaps best known for their supporting role in layered desserts, but they are quite good on their own.

To create the ladyfinger's signature shape, a pastry bag is filled with sponge batter and fitted with a plain piping tip. The batter is then piped into long ovals, or "fingers," on parchment paper. The unbaked cookies get a double dusting of confectioners' sugar to give the baked cookie a crispy exterior, contrasting with the soft, spongy interior.

---

3 eggs, separated
6 tablespoons granulated sugar
¾ cup all-purpose flour

2 tablespoons cornstarch
6 tablespoons confectioners' sugar

---

1. Preheat the oven to 350°F. Lightly brush 2 baking sheets with canola or safflower oil and line with parchment paper (the oil will cause the paper to adhere to the pan). Fit a pastry bag with a large plain tip. (You can also use a plastic zip-top bag without a piping tip and snip the corner after it is filled with the batter.)

2. Beat the egg whites using a handheld electric mixer until stiff peaks form. Gradually add the granulated sugar and continue beating until the egg whites become glossy and smooth.

3. In a small bowl, beat the egg yolks lightly with a fork. Fold them into the meringue with a rubber spatula.

4. Sift the flour and cornstarch over the mixture and fold very gently until just mixed. Do not overfold; otherwise, the batter will deflate and you will have flat, nonspongy cookies.

5. Fill the pastry bag or plastic zip-top bag with sponge batter.

6. Pipe the batter into 4-inch-long ovals.

7. Sift half the confectioners' sugar over the ladyfingers and wait for 5 minutes. The sugar will pearl, or look wet and glisten. Now sift the remaining sugar over the cookies. This helps to give the ladyfingers their characteristic crispness.

8. Holding the parchment paper in place with your thumb, lift one side of the baking sheet and gently tap it on the work surface to remove excess confectioners' sugar.

9. Bake the ladyfingers for 10 minutes. Rotate the sheets and bake for another 5 minutes or until they puff up and turn lightly golden brown.

10. Cool the ladyfingers on the baking sheets for about 5 minutes. Transfer them to a cooling rack with a spatula while still warm. Cool completely; store in an airtight container until ready to use.

TUILES

YIELD: Approximately 30 cookies

These French cookies, pronounced *tweel*, are named for their resemblance to French roof tiles. They are made from stencil paste, a versatile batter from which many different sculptural elements can be created, from cookie spoons to edible bowls.

---

3 egg whites
1 cup confectioners' sugar
¾ cup flour
Gel food coloring (optional)
4 tablespoons butter, melted

½ teaspoon vanilla extract, or seeds of 1 vanilla bean
Vegetable shortening for greasing the cookie sheet

---

1. In a medium bowl, whisk the egg whites and confectioners' sugar together until smooth.

2. Whisk the flour into the egg-white mixture until just combined.

3. Tint the batter with gel food coloring, if desired.

4. Using a wooden spoon, gently stir in the melted butter and vanilla extract. When the mixture is well combined, cover and refrigerate for 30 minutes.

5. Preheat the oven to 400°F. Grease a cookie sheet with shortening, and line with parchment paper. Grease a rolling pin and place it on a work surface in close proximity to the oven.

6. Spoon 2- to 3-teaspoon portions of batter at least 6 inches apart onto the parchment paper, about 6 cookies to 1 sheet.

7. With a small offset spatula, spread the batter thinly into 2- to 3-inch rounds.

8. Bake for 5 to 8 minutes.

9. Working out of the oven, gently run an offset spatula underneath each cookie and transfer it to the greased rolling pin, gently

pressing the cookie to shape it into a rounded "tile" over the surface of the rolling pin. The cookies will harden quickly, so you must shape them while they are still warm.

VARIATIONS

Shaped *tuiles*: Make a stencil by tracing a shape onto heavy-grade craft paper, thin cardboard, or even the plastic lids from takeout containers (which have the added benefit of being washable). Cut the shape out with an X-Acto blade, then scrape the batter across the stencil into the crevices.

Tulipes: *Tuiles* can also be molded into containers that can hold berries or other fillings. Using two ramekins or stackable fluted molds lightly greased with shortening, carefully place the warm round cookie into the bowl of one ramekin. Gently stack the other greased ramekin on top, pressing lightly to create a bowl shape. Let stand until the cookie is crisp. These *tuile* bowls are called tulips because they are ruffled, like the petals on a tulip.

no stencil required!

A. Spread the batter with an off-set spatula. **B.** Remove the template to reveal the shape. **C.** The batter can also be spread with an off-set spatula into 2- to 3-inch free-form rounds. **D.** Press the cookies over a rolling pin to shape them. **E.** To shape round *tuiles* into containers, press them between two cups. **F.** Gently remove the cups.

MACARONS

YIELD: 12 sandwich cookies or 24 individual shells

French *macarons* are petite sandwich cookies made of meringue, confectioners' sugar, and almond flour. They may not be the easiest cookies to make, but they just might be the prettiest. As they bake, a frill forms around the bottom edge of the cookie that is often called a *pied*, or "foot." This is the result of careful sifting, whipping, folding, and baking. If any of these tasks is mishandled, the distinctive foot will fail to develop.

Don't be discouraged if your first batches are unsuccessful. Even experienced bakers and pastry chefs have experienced *macaron* failure.

---

1 cup confectioners' sugar
¾ cup almond flour
2 egg whites, at room temperature

Pinch of cream of tartar
¼ cup superfine sugar
Gel food coloring (optional)

---

1. Line two baking sheets with parchment paper. Fit a pastry bag with a ¾-inch plain tip (or use a zip-top plastic bag without a tip and snip the corner after filling).

2. Add the confectioners' sugar and almond flour to the bowl of a food processor and pulse until well combined.

3. Using a hand mixer, beat the egg whites at medium speed until frothy. Stop the mixer and add the cream of tartar. Start the mixer again and continue beating at medium speed until soft peaks form. Reduce the speed to low and gradually add the superfine sugar, 1 tablespoon at a time. Increase the speed to high, and beat until stiff peaks form. The finished meringue should have a smooth, shiny appearance.

4. Sift the almond flour mixture over the egg whites and fold together with a rubber spatula until just mixed. At this point you may add a drop or two of food coloring to tint the batter. Continue to fold the mixture until it has loosened considerably and falls in a ribbon from the spatula.

5. Transfer the batter to the pastry bag.

6. Pipe 1½-inch rounds approximately 1 inch apart on the prepared baking sheets. As you pipe, drag the pastry tip to the side of the rounds to avoid forming peaks. The piped rounds will spread slightly.

7. Tap the bottom of each sheet on the work surface to release trapped air bubbles.

8. Let stand at room temperature for 15 to 30 minutes to dry. Preheat the oven to 375°F.

9. Just before putting the pans in the oven, reduce the oven temperature to 325°F. Bake for 10 minutes, rotating the baking pan halfway through the baking time, until the *macaron* are puffed and have formed the frill, or foot, around the bottom edge of the cookie. The feet may deflate slightly after the pan is removed from the oven—this is normal and should be expected.

10. Let the *macaron* shells cool completely on the baking sheets. Carefully peel them away from the parchment paper.

11. Select two same-size *macaron* shells to sandwich together with 1 teaspoon filling.

TIPS

- If you don't have time to let your egg whites come to room temperature, you can place them in a microwave-safe bowl and heat them in the microwave for 10 to 15 seconds. Microwaves vary in strength, so be extra careful to not cook the egg whites.

- *Macaron* shells can be frozen for up to 3 months. Thaw completely at room temperature before filling.

- Use insulated baking pans (such as T-Fal Air-Bake) or use an additional cookie sheet under the pan of piped *macarons* to ensure that the shells do not over-bake.

FLAVOR VARIATIONS

The following powdered ingredients can be sifted in with the almond flour and confectioners' sugar.

- Chocolate: Remove 3 tablespoons almond flour and replace with 3 tablespoons unsweetened cocoa powder.

- Cinnamon: Add 1 teaspoon ground cinnamon.

- Coffee: Add 1 teaspoon espresso powder.

- Matcha: Add 1 to 2 teaspoons matcha tea powder.

FILLING IDEAS

- Buttercream
- Chocolate ganache
- Jelly or jam
- Lemon curd
- Marshmallow cream
- Nut butter
- Pastry cream

EMBELLISHMENTS

Just after the *macaron* batter is piped, the rounds may be sprinkled with candy, seeds, nuts, or spice powders for decorative effect.

- Garnish ideas:
- Black pepper
- Black sesame seeds
- Cocoa powder or cocoa nibs
- Crushed freeze-dried berries or other fruit
- Ground pistachios, peanuts, or other nuts
- Nonpareils, sprinkles, candy confetti, or jimmies
- Baked *macaron* shells can be painted with a mixture of vodka and gel food coloring. Simply mix ½ tsp gel food coloring with one or two drops of vodka from a clean eyedropper.

MACARON TROUBLESHOOTING GUIDE

Macarons did not develop feet:

- The piped rounds have sat too long and have become too hard to form a foot when baked. Dry them for no longer than 30 minutes. For most nonhumid climates, 15 minutes is sufficient.

- The oven temperature was too low. If you suspect your oven heats too low or too high, purchase an oven thermometer to gauge the accuracy of your oven.

- The batter was not folded enough.

- The meringue was not beaten long enough.

Macarons developed feet, but became lopsided and runny:

- The oven was too hot.

- The sugar was not fine enough. Do not substitute regular white sugar when making *macarons*; you must use superfine sugar.

Macarons lack gloss and are dry:

- The batter was not folded enough.

Macarons have oily spots on the surface:

- The batter was over-mixed.

a little goes a long way

this is the "foot"

A. Once the almond flour and egg whites are just mixed, add a drop or two of gel food coloring.
B. Fold in the food coloring, scooping from the bottom of the bowl and folding over. The mixture is ready when it falls from the spatula in a thick ribbon. C. Pipe the batter into 1½-inch rounds on the parchment paper. D. Pipe rounds approximately 1 inch apart. E. Bake until "foot" forms around the bottom edge of the cookie.

CAKES

· ·

THINGS TO KEEP IN MIND

▨ Read the recipe in its entirety before beginning any cake project.

▨ Measure all ingredients accurately. Spoon—don't scoop—dry ingredients into measuring cups, and then swipe a straightedge, such as the back of a knife or icing spatula, across the top of the measuring cup to level the ingredients.

▨ Sift dry ingredients to prevent lumps in, and to better aerate, the batter.

▨ Make sure the cake pan is properly lined. Pans used for sponge cakes and other light batters that contain whipped egg whites can be left unlined, but they need to be greased and lightly floured.

▨ Use an oven thermometer. If your cake bakes more quickly than the recipe indicates, your oven may be too hot. Alternatively, if your cake takes longer to bake than the recipe indicates, your oven may not be hot enough. Using an oven thermometer can help you best gauge the temperature of your oven. This will help you avoid undesirable results, such as overbrowned and undercooked cakes.

LINING BAKING PANS

Cake pans are lined in different ways according to the type of cake batter being used. Pans for cakes with light batters with short cooking times are sometimes left unlined and instead greased and lightly floured. Pans for dense batters need to be greased and doubly lined so the cake bakes evenly and does not stick to the pan.

LINING A STANDARD 9-INCH CAKE PAN

Place the bottom of the pan over a piece of parchment paper and draw around the outside with a pencil; cut out the circle with scissors. Coat the pan evenly with vegetable shortening, using a pastry brush or paper towel. Lay the parchment circle in the bottom of the pan. Smooth out air pockets as you flatten the parchment. Grease the paper with shortening. Fill the lined pan with batter.

LINING A JELLY ROLL PAN

Place the bottom of the pan on a large sheet of parchment. Cut the parchment down to 1 inch larger than the pan base on all sides. Cut the paper from each corner up to the corner of the pan. Grease the pan and set the parchment in the bottom of the pan, pressing the edges in.

LINING A DEEP CAKE OR SPRINGFORM PAN

Place the pan on two stacked sheets of parchment paper. Draw around the base with a pencil. Cut out the shape from both pieces of parchment and set aside. Measure the circumference and height of the pan. Cut a strip of double-layer parchment about 1 inch higher than the pan's rim, making sure it's long enough to wrap around the inside of the pan. Grease the bottom and sides of the pan with shortening and fit the double-layer strip on the interior sides of the pan, allowing it to stick to the shortening. You may need to grease between the layers so the inner layer is flush and stands upright. Fit the double-layer circle into the base. Grease the bottom and sides of the paper, smoothing out any wrinkles.

In order to ensure that your deep cake doesn't overbrown, you also need to line the outside of the cake pan. First, lay an old tea towel soaked with water and lightly wrung out inside a jelly roll pan. Then set the lined cake pan on the tea towel. Wrap another damp tea towel around the outside of the cake pan and tie it with baker's twine to secure. This step ensures that the cake will bake evenly and that the outside edges and bottom of the cake will not overbrown before the middle of the cake is done.

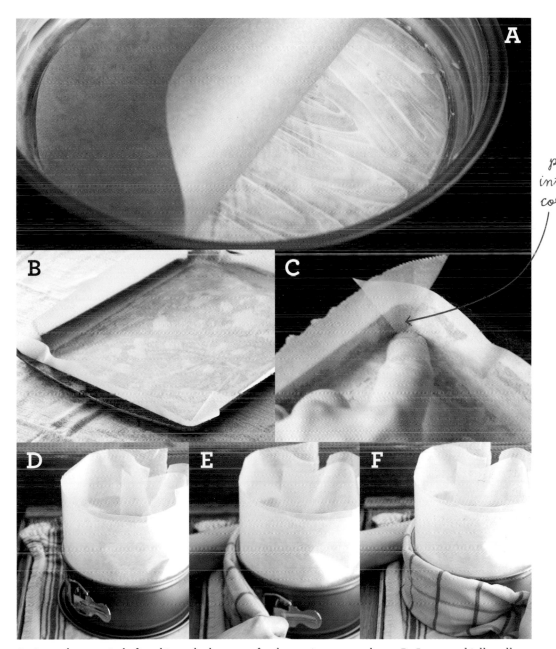

press into the corner!

A. A parchment circle fitted into the bottom of a shortening-greased pan. B. A greased jelly roll pan lined with parchment paper. C. Snip the parchment paper down to the corners of the pan, then press them down with one finger. D. A lined springform pan on a towel-lined pan. E. Fold a wet tea towel to the height of the side of the springform pan. F. Wrap the tea towel around the springform pan and secure it with baker's twine.

BUTTER CAKE WITH SIMPLE SYRUP

YIELD: 7½ cups cake batter; makes 3 (8- or 9-inch) cakes; approximately 2½ cups simple syrup

This dense butter cake recipe provides a perfect base for your choice of fillings or frostings. It yields a large quantity of batter, so it is ideal for large celebration and tiered wedding cakes. Flavored simple syrups, which are brushed onto completely cooled, uniced cakes, can be used to impart more moisture and added flavor.

BUTTER CAKE

- ¾ pound (3 sticks) butter, softened
- 2½ cups sugar
- 5 eggs, at room temperature
- 1 tablespoon vanilla extract, or choice of flavoring (see Variations)
- 3 cups all-purpose flour
- 1 teaspoon baking powder
- ¼ teaspoon salt
- 1 cup whole milk, at room temperature

SIMPLE SYRUP

- 1¼ cups granulated sugar
- 1 cup water
- Choice of flavoring (see Variations)

Make the butter cake:

1. Preheat the oven to 350°F. Grease 3 (8- or 9-inch) cake pans with vegetable shortening and line the bottoms with parchment.

2. In the bowl of a stand mixer fitted with the paddle attachment, cream the butter and sugar until lightened in color and fluffy, 4 to 5 minutes.

3. Add the eggs, one at a time, mixing well after each addition.

4. Mix in the vanilla extract.

5. Sift together the flour, baking powder, and salt.

6. Add the flour mixture to the butter mixture in 3 additions, alternating with the milk; begin and end with the flour mixture, and beat after each addition until well combined. Beat until the batter is smooth and thoroughly combined.

7. Pour the batter into the prepared pans.

8. Bake for 30 to 50 minutes, according to the size of your pan. Cakes made in standard 9-inch round cake pans will bake in 35 to 40 minutes; 8-inch cakes will bake in 30 to 35 minutes. The cake is done when a skewer inserted in the center of the cake comes out clean.

9. Cool for 10 minutes in the pan. Loosen the sides with a small, thin offset spatula. Invert the cake layers, remove the parchment rounds, and transfer the cakes to cooling racks. Cool completely before decorating.

Make the simple syrup:

1. While the cake is baking, place the sugar and water in a medium saucepan over medium heat. Heat until sugar granules have dissolved.

2. Increase the heat to medium-high and bring to a boil.

3. Remove from the heat and let cool slightly.

4. Add the flavoring.

5. Use as soon as the syrup is lukewarm or store in the refrigerator until needed.

6. Apply cooled syrup to the tops of cakes with a large pastry brush, being careful not to tear the cake, until the cake is well moistened but not soggy. Proceed with icing the cake with your choice of buttercream.

CAKE VARIATIONS

Citrus Cake: Add the zest of 4 oranges, lemons, or limes to the creamed butter.

Vanilla Cake: Add the seeds of 2 vanilla beans to the creamed butter.

SYRUP VARIATIONS

Add flavorings to cooled syrup, beginning with the amounts listed here; taste and adjust flavorings by adding more until the desired flavor is reached.

- Hazelnut—1 tablespoon Frangelico liqueur
- Lemon—1 tablespoon Limoncello liqueur or 2 teaspoons lemon extract
- Mint—1 to 2 teaspoons peppermint extract
- Orange—1 tablespoon Grand Marnier liqueur or 2 teaspoons orange extract
- Vanilla—seeds from one vanilla bean or 2 teaspoons vanilla extract

SERVING SUGGESTIONS

Black and White Cake: Bake the vanilla cake variation, split each cake horizontally, and fill with whipped ganache. Ice the cake with chocolate-flavored American buttercream.

Citrus Cake: Bake the citrus cake variation, brush with Limoncello syrup, and fill and ice with citrus-flavored Swiss buttercream.

Hazelnut Cake: Bake the vanilla cake variation, brush with Frangelico syrup, and fill and ice with hazelnut-flavored Swiss buttercream. Garnish the cake with toasted whole and chopped hazelnuts.

CHOCOLATE CAKE

YIELD: 2 (9-inch) cakes

There are so many things I love about this cake, but what sets it apart from other chocolate cakes is the generous dose of coffee that is mixed into the batter. It really wakes up the chocolate flavor without giving it an overwhelming taste of coffee. Use the best-quality chocolate and cocoa powder you can find for a delicious result.

Note: If you plan to serve this to young children or to people who are sensitive to caffeine, you can substitute low-fat chocolate milk for the coffee.

---

3 ounces semisweet chocolate, finely chopped
1½ cups strong coffee, freshly brewed and piping hot
2½ cups all-purpose flour
3 cups sugar
1½ cups unsweetened cocoa powder

2 teaspoons baking soda
¾ teaspoon baking powder
1¼ teaspoons salt
3 eggs
¾ cup canola oil
1½ cups buttermilk
¾ teaspoon vanilla extract

---

1. Preheat the oven to 300°F. Grease 2 (9-inch) pans with shortening. Line the bottoms of the pans with rounds of parchment paper and grease the paper.

2. Put the chocolate in a heatproof bowl and pour the hot coffee over it. Stir the mixture, pausing intermittently to allow the chocolate to melt. When the mixture is smooth, set it aside to cool.

3. Sift together the flour, sugar, cocoa powder, baking soda, baking powder, and salt.

4. In a large bowl, beat the eggs with a handheld mixer until thickened and slightly lightened in color.

5. Add the canola oil, buttermilk, vanilla extract, and cooled coffee-chocolate mixture to the eggs. Beat again with the handheld mixer until combined.

6. Add the flour mixture and beat on medium speed until just combined well.

7. Pour the batter into the prepared pans and bake for 50 minutes to 1 hour, until a toothpick or skewer inserted in the center comes out clean.

8. Let the layers cool completely while still resting inside the pans. Run an offset spatula around the edge of the cakes, invert and remove the pans, and remove the parchment.

9. Frost with your favorite icing.

SERVING SUGGESTIONS

Chocolate-Orange: Brush the cake layers with orange or Grand Marnier syrup and fill and ice with orange Swiss buttercream.

Death by Chocolate: Ice with whipped chocolate ganache and garnish with chocolate shavings—dark, milk, or white, or a combination

FINANCIERS

YIELD: 12 *financiers* or 16 mini-muffins

Browned butter gives these almond tea cakes a refined flavor and a beautiful golden color. They are traditionally baked in rectangular tart pans and said to resemble bars of gold, hence the name *financier*. These days, it's perfectly acceptable to bake them in any form you deem fit. Use a mini-muffin tin if you aren't inclined to buy specialty pans. Top them with fresh fruit and whipped cream for a more indulgent treat.

½ cup almond flour or finely ground almonds
¼ pound (1 stick) butter
¼ cup all-purpose flour
¾ cup confectioners' sugar

⅛ teaspoon salt
3 egg whites
Seeds of 1 vanilla bean
Fresh berries or other small pieces of fruit (optional)

1. Preheat the oven to 350°F.

2. Place the almond flour on a parchment-lined baking sheet and toast it in the oven for 6 to 8 minutes, or until lightly browned and fragrant. Remove the almond flour from the oven and let cool.

3. Increase the oven temperature to 400°F. Place 12 tart molds on a baking sheet (you will grease them with the leftover browned butter) or line a mini-muffin tin with 12 paper cupcake liners. Line a mesh sieve with cheesecloth or a coffee filter and place it over a small bowl.

4. In a small saucepan, melt the butter over medium heat.

5. Once the butter is melted, increase the heat slightly and allow the butter to come to a boil. Swirl the pan occasionally; do not stir. As the butter boils, you will notice foam forming on the butter's surface, and the milk solids will settle to the bottom of the pan. Continue cooking until the milk solids in the bottom of the pan

turn a light golden brown. Do not overcook—butter can easily burn and become bitter.

6. Immediately remove from the heat and strain through the mesh sieve lined with cheesecloth or a coffee filter; discard the butter solids that collect. Let cool to room temperature. You will use only ⅓ cup of the browned butter in the batter. Use the leftover melted butter to grease the molds using a pastry brush.

7. In a large bowl, whisk together the flour, almond flour, confectioners' sugar, and salt.

8. Make a small well in the center of the flour mixture and fold in the egg whites, vanilla bean seeds, and ⅓ cup cooled browned butter.

9. Fill each mold and bake for 12 minutes. If using fruit, bake the mini-cakes for 4 minutes and remove from the oven. Place a few berries on top of each *financier*. Return the molds to the oven and bake a further 5 to 7 minutes or until the *financiers* have become light brown on top and are springy to the touch.

browned butter—nutty and delicious!

A. Make a well in the center of the flour, then add the wet ingredients. **B.** Almond flour toasted to a golden color. **C.** Take the *financiers* out of the tart pans and turn them so they can cool on top of the pans.

10. Remove the *financiers* from the oven and let cool on a wire rack before removing them from molds. These are best eaten the same day they are made. The batter will keep for several days in the refrigerator.

VARIATIONS

Lemon *Financiers*: Add the zest of 2 lemons to the batter in place of the vanilla seeds.

Orange *Financiers*: Add the zest of 1 orange to the batter in place of the vanilla seeds.

GÉNOISE SPONGE CAKE

YIELD: 1 (9-inch) cake

Génoise is a classic whisked sponge cake that has a firm texture and is perfect for slicing into thin layers. Its resilient sponginess makes a sturdy base to build fancy desserts and many-layered gateaux. Fill it with your choice of curds, creams, custards, fruit, and nuts.

4 eggs
½ cup superfine sugar
3 tablespoons butter, melted and cooled
¾ cup plus 2 tablespoons all-purpose flour
Choice of flavoring (see Variations)

1. Preheat the oven to 350°F. Grease a 9-inch cake pan with shortening and line the bottom with parchment. Grease the parchment.

2. Fill a medium saucepan ⅓ full of water and bring to a simmer over medium-high heat.

3. In a heatproof bowl, beat the eggs and sugar together with a handheld mixer. When they are well incorporated, place the bowl over the pan of simmering water and continue beating the mixture until it is thick and pale.

Note: The heatproof bowl should be large enough to sit on top of the pan, so it does not touch the water and does not sit in the pan.

4. Remove the bowl from the saucepan. Continue beating the mixture until it has cooled and leaves a trail of batter when the beaters are lifted out of the bowl.

5. At the edge of the batter bowl, carefully pour the melted butter into the mixture.

6. Sift the flour over the batter and add the desired flavoring.

7. Fold the contents of the bowl together with a rubber spatula. Do this gently to avoid deflating the batter.

8. Pour the mixture into the prepared pan. Bake for 30 to 40 minutes, or until a toothpick tester comes out clean.

9. Cool for 5 minutes in the pan. Invert and remove the pan, remove the parchment, and cool the cake completely on a rack before decorating.

Note: This recipe can be doubled for a 2-layer cake.

VARIATIONS

Chocolate: Add 2 ounces melted semisweet chocolate to the batter after folding in the flour and melted butter. Slice the cake in half horizontally with a serrated knife. Fill the layers and ice with whipped chocolate ganache.

Citrus: Add 2 teaspoons grated lemon, lime, or orange rind to the batter. Slice the cake in half horizontally with a serrated knife. Fill the cake with fresh orange and grapefruit segments. Ice the cake with whipped cream, and refrigerate.

Vanilla: Add the seeds of 1 vanilla bean or 1 teaspoon vanilla extract to the batter.

this is the batter trail

A. Beat the egg mixture over a pan of simmering water. **B.** The mixture is ready when a thick trail of it remains on the surface. **C.** Fold flour into the egg mixture. **D.** You can top a slice of *génoise* with Blackberry Curd (see page 192) for extra goodness.

MADEIRA CAKE

YIELD: Small batch, 1 (7-inch) square cake or 1 (8-inch) round cake OR large batch, 1 (10-inch) square cake or 1 (11 inch) round cake

Madeira cake dates back to nineteenth-century England. It is a very sturdy cake with a dense crumb but, surprisingly, does not have *Madeira*, a fortified wine, in the ingredients. Rather, glasses of it were served alongside slices of this moist, delicious dessert.

Madeira cake is, hands down, the best cake for carving. It can be cut, stacked, and shaped without crumbling or splitting. A good-quality serrated knife should be used for *Madeira* cake projects. Both small- and large-batch recipes can be doubled to suit the needs of your cake design.

Note: A hand mixer may be used for small batch *Madeira* batter. A stand mixer should be used for large-batch *Madeira* batter.

SMALL BATCH
- 3 cups all-purpose flour
- 1½ teaspoons baking powder
- 1¼ cup sugar
- ½ pound plus 4 tablespoons (2½ sticks) butter, softened
- 3 eggs, at room temperature
- 3 tablespoons milk, plus more as needed
- Choice of flavoring (see Variations)

LARGE BATCH
- 5 cups all-purpose flour
- 3 teaspoons baking powder
- 2¼ cups sugar
- 1 pound plus 4 tablespoons (4½ sticks) butter, softened
- 10 eggs, at room temperature
- 4½ tablespoons milk, plus more as needed
- Choice of flavoring (see Variations)

---

1. Preheat the oven to 325°F. Grease a pan with vegetable shortening and line the bottom and sides with parchment. Grease the parchment.

2. In a mixing bowl, sift together the flour and baking powder.

3. Add the sugar, butter, eggs, and milk. Blend on low speed with an electric mixer. Increase the speed until a thick batter has formed. Add additional milk, 1 tablespoon at a time, if the mixture is too thick.

4. Add the desired flavoring and mix until well combined.

5. Scoop the batter out of the mixing bowl and into the prepared pan. Spread as evenly as possible with an offset spatula.

6. Give the cake pan two good raps on the work surface to remove any trapped air bubbles.

7. Bake the cake until a toothpick or skewer inserted in the center comes out clean: 1 to 1¼ hours for small-batch *Madeira* and 2 to 2¼ hours for large-batch *Madeira*.

8. Let cool completely in the pan. Turn the cake out of the pan, remove the parchment, and store in an airtight container until ready for use.

Note: For best results, let the completely cooled cake stand in an airtight container or wrapped in plastic wrap for 6 hours before carving. This allows the cake's texture to settle and makes for more precise carving.

A. Line the edges and bottom of pan. **B.** *Madeira* batter will be thick. **C.** Spread the batter to the sides of the pan with an off-set spatula until it is even.

VARIATIONS

Citrus—For small batch, add 1 teaspoon lemon, lime, or orange juice and 1 teaspoon zest; for large batch, add 2 tablespoons juice and 2 tablespoons zest.

Coconut—For small batch, add 1 cup desiccated coconut; for large batch, add 3 cups.

Fruit—For small batch, add 1 scant cup candied fruit; for large batch, add 3 cups.

Vanilla—For small batch, add 1 vanilla bean or 1 teaspoon vanilla extract; for large batch, add 3 vanilla beans or 1 tablespoon extract.

SERVING SUGGESTIONS

Boston Cream Pie—Slice the cake in half horizontally and fill with vanilla pastry cream (see page 59). Drizzle the top and sides of the cake with cooled liquid chocolate ganache. Note: Yes, it's really a cake!

Chocolate Mint Cake—Slice the cake in half horizontally with a serrated knife and brush both pieces with mint-flavored simple syrup. Ice with chocolate Swiss buttercream.

Raspberry Shortcake—Slice the cake in half horizontally, brush with plain simple syrup, and fill with fresh raspberries and whipped cream. Ice the cake with additional whipped cream, or dust the cake with confectioners' sugar.

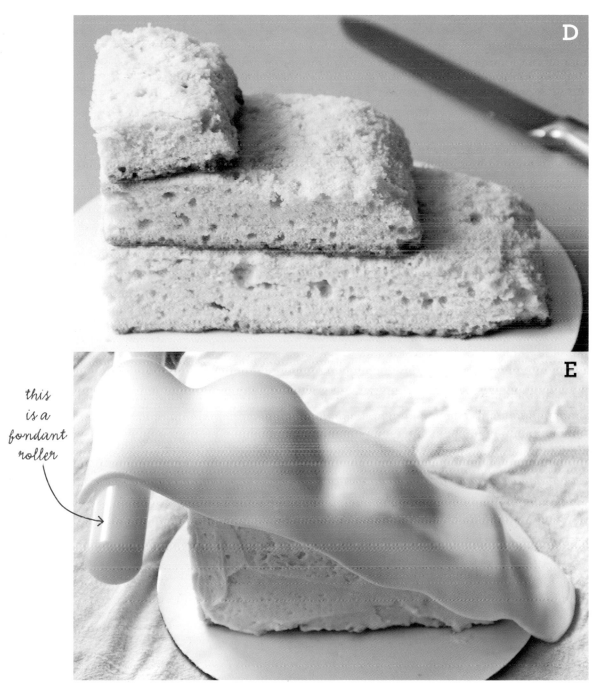

this is a fondant roller

D. *Madeira* cake can be carved and stacked. **E.** This sturdy cake can then be frosted with butter-cream and covered in rolled fondant (sugar paste) to create smooth, flowing lines.

CANDIES

·····································

THINGS TO KEEP IN MIND

▪ You can buy a basic candy or deep-fry thermometer for as little as six dollars, or you may want to spend a little more for a digital one that has an alarm. Either way, I highly recommend investing in one. It can be difficult to determine the different stages of boiled candy (from soft ball to hard crack) if you are just beginning your candy-making journey. If you plan on tempering chocolate, it's a good idea to have a chocolate thermometer as well. These register a temperature range from around 80°F to 120°F, the ideal range needed to temper chocolate properly.

▪ Making caramel will require your undivided attention. Don't start any other projects with time constraints while making caramel—sugar browns quickly and can burn if left unattended. Sugar will continue to cook and caramelize in a hot pan even after it is removed from the heat. If your caramel is cooking quickly and has reached the desired depth of color, you can stop the cooking by dipping the bottom of the pan in cool water.

▪ Use extreme caution when boiling candy. There's nothing worse than getting molten candy stuck to your skin. It cannot be removed quickly or easily and can cause very serious burns. It's a good idea to have a small bowl of ice water near the stove when boiling sugar. If it splatters or spills on you, quickly immerse the area in ice water to minimize burning.

▪ Making candy is one of the most scientifically quantifiable dessert-making processes, as long as you have a candy thermometer. Here is a guide to the temperature ranges at which the different types of candy are achieved.

Candy-Cooking Temperature Guide

Soft ball	234–240°F
Firm ball	242–248°F
Hard ball	250–268°F
Soft crack	270–290°F
Hard crack	300–310°F
Caramel	320–338°F

Note: While caramel has a temperature range, there is no better way to gauge whether the transformation has happened than standing over the boiling pot or pan, watching for that perfect amber color to develop.

CRÈME CANDIES

YIELD: 120 to 150 candies

Sweet *crème* candy dough is one of the easiest candy recipes you will ever make—no thermometer required! The dough is best when flavored with extracts and dipped into candy coating or almond bark. You can shape the candies by hand or use a candy mold for a fancier presentation.

Code candy by shape, and you'll be able to tell what flavor candy you have after they are dipped. (Or don't and be surprised!)

½ cup unsalted butter
1 teaspoon salt
⅔ cup sweetened condensed milk
5 to 5½ cups confectioners' sugar, plus
   additional if needed

Choice of flavorings (see Variations)
Liquid food coloring
2 pounds candy coating, chocolate
   bark or almond bark

---

1. Line 2 cookie sheets with parchment paper (or 4, if you have them).

2. In a mixer fitted with the paddle attachment, cream the margarine and salt on medium speed.

3. Blend in the sweetened condensed milk until smooth.

4. Add 5 cups of the confectioners' sugar and mix until a uniformly stiff dough forms. If the dough is sticky, add the remaining ½ cup confectioners' sugar.

5. Gather the dough into a ball and place it in an airtight container until ready to divide. The dough should not be sticky; if it is, knead more confectioners' sugar into the dough, 2 tablespoons at a time.

6. Separate the dough into approximately 4 (1-cup) portions and place in separate bowls.

7. Create an indentation in the middle of the dough with your fingers and pour in ½ teaspoon desired flavoring.

8. Knead the dough in the bowl with your hands (the dough will be sticky at first) until all the flavoring has been absorbed. You may also knead in 2 drops of food coloring at this stage. Wear plastic gloves to prevent staining your hands.

9. Shape the dough into pieces with your fingers (squares, balls, rectangles) and place on the prepared cookie sheet.

10. Chill the shaped candies in the refrigerator for about 30 minutes.

11. Melt candy coating or almond bark in the microwave at 30-second intervals until smooth. Using a fork, dip the chilled candy *crèmes* in the melted candy, and using another fork, slide them onto parchment paper. Allow to dry 10 to 15 minutes or until coating is rigid and has lost its gloss..

12. Store the candies in an airtight container.

Note: The candy will keep for up to 1 month, covered, at room temperature.

VARIATIONS

Extracts: use ½ teaspoon extract per 1 cup candy dough:

- Lemon: Flavor the dough with lemon extract and tint with yellow food coloring.
- Maple: Flavor the dough with maple extract.
- Mint: Flavor the dough with peppermint extract and tint with green food coloring, or leave untinted and shape into a disc. Dip in chocolate bark for a homemade mint patty.

- Orange: Flavor the dough with orange extract and tint with orange food coloring.

Filled candies:

- Cherry: Drain and pat dry maraschino cherries, wrap them in candy dough, and dip them in almond bark.
- Walnut: Flavor the candy dough with black walnut extract and wrap candy around a walnut half.

A. *Crème* candy dough will be thick and slightly crumbly. **B.** The oval shapes of the candies represent their black walnut flavor. **C.** Square lemon *crème* candies are tinted yellow as an indication of their flavor.

MODELING CHOCOLATE

YIELD: 12 oz. of clay, approximately 1⅓ cups

This simple formula for modeling chocolate is easily the most versatile recipe I've found yet. It can be sculpted by hand, cut into shapes, or pressed into candy molds.

1 (10-ounce) package semisweet chocolate chips
⅓ cup light corn syrup

1. Heat the chocolate chips in the microwave at full power in a microwave-safe bowl at 30-second intervals, stirring thoroughly after each heating.

2. When the chips are completely melted, add the corn syrup and stir until the mixture becomes thick; the chocolate will lose its shiny appearance.

3. Spread the mixture on a large piece of wax paper with a spatula and top with another piece of wax paper. Gently even out with a rolling pin or by pressing to a ½-inch thickness.

4. Let dry 2 to 3 hours.

5. Remove the paper from the surface and knead the chocolate until pliable and puttylike. Chocolate sculptures will harden when left at room temperature.

6. Wrap unused "clay" tightly in plastic wrap and store in an airtight container. Discard after 3 months.

VARIATIONS

For cut shapes: Skip the kneading and use cookie cutters to cut pieces as if you were making sugar cookies. Use the chocolate shapes to decorate cakes and cookies.

For molded candies: Dust candy molds with unsweetened cocoa powder. Press chocolate into molds and remove. Let dry at room temperature until hardened.

the possibilities are endless!

A. Stir the melted chocolate and corn syrup together until the mixture is thick. **B.** Soften the modeling chocolate by hand-kneading it. **C.** Create simple shapes, such as graduated circles that can be stacked. **D.** A sphinx sculpted from modeling chocolate and coated with silver luster dust.

HARD CANDY

YIELD: Approximately 100 candies cut into small pieces

This recipe can be used to make a variety of hard candies, including my all-time favorite—lollipops! I love the jewel-like appearance it has when cut into squares with a pizza cutter.

2 cups sugar
⅔ cup corn syrup
⅔ cup water
½ to 1 dram bottle (¾ teaspoon) flavoring oil
Food coloring (optional)

1. If you are using a candy mold, lightly grease it with cooking spray. If you are not using a mold, grease a baking sheet with vegetable shortening and line it with parchment. Grease the parchment paper.

2. Stir together the sugar, corn syrup, and water in a small saucepan and clip a candy thermometer to the side of the pan.

3. Bring the mixture to a boil over high heat. Continue to heat without stirring until the bubbling mixture reaches the hard-crack stage (302°F). Remove pan from heat.

4. Stir in the flavoring oil and food coloring. Be extra careful because the mixture will bubble and sputter with these additions.

5. When the mixture has stopped bubbling, pour it into molds or onto a baking sheet and let harden. If you are not using molds, break the candy into pieces or cut it with an oil-sprayed pizza wheel before the candy hardens.

6. Wrap the cooled candies in wax paper and store in an airtight container.

HARD CANDY COATING

YIELD: Approximately 2½ cups, enough for 8 to 10 small apples, 20 crab apples, or ½ pound grapes or cherries

This is a great candy coating for small apples, crab apples, small pears, cherries, or grapes. It makes a beautiful presentation or centerpiece but must be consumed within 1 day, as the fruit can weep, causing the hard sugar to begin to dissolve. Be sure the fruit is very clean and completely dry, as moisture is the enemy of any hard candy coating.

½ cup light corn syrup
1 cup water
3 cups sugar
1 dram bottle (¾ teaspoon) flavoring oil

1. Grease a jelly roll pan with vegetable shortening.

2. Wash and dry the fruit thoroughly.

3. Insert an ice pop stick or skewer into large fruits and lift to make sure the fruit can be picked up and held securely without falling off. Cherries and grapes can be held by the stem to dip.

4. Combine the corn syrup, water, and sugar in a medium saucepan with a handle. Clip a candy thermometer to the edge of the saucepan.

5. Heat on medium-high until the sugar has dissolved.

6. Increase the heat and bring the mixture to a boil. The sugar mixture will take 20 to 25 minutes to reach 302°F on a candy thermometer. This is known as the hard-crack stage.

7. Once the hard-crack stage has been reached, remove the pan from the burner and add the flavoring. Mix well.

8. Dip the fruit, one at a time, into the candy, swirling until completely coated in syrup. Hold the fruit above the saucepan to let excess candy drain off. As you work, you may need to tilt the saucepan to pool the candy to one side. This will help ensure that the entire quantity of fruit gets a full coating as your mixture gets lower.

9. Place the candy-coated fruit on the prepared jelly roll pan and allow to harden.

HARD CARAMEL

YIELD: Approximately 1 cup of liquid caramel

Hard caramel is a candy garnish that delivers on flavor and is sure to impress. It is used to hold together elaborate desserts; it can be drizzled into shapes, pulled into ribbons, or curled around a spoon handle for corkscrew embellishments. Remember—cooked sugar is extremely hot and will cause serious burns if touched before it cools. It's wise to keep ice water nearby just in case you accidentally touch it; you can quickly dunk your hand in the water to minimize any burns. Be careful!

1 cup sugar
½ teaspoon lemon juice

1. Partially fill a large heatproof bowl with cold water. The bowl needs to be large enough to comfortably accommodate the bottom of a medium saucepan.

2. Combine the sugar and lemon juice in a medium saucepan.

3. Stir until the sugar resembles wet sand.

4. Place the pan over medium heat and cook without stirring until the sugar begins to melt around the sides of the pan.

5. Stir the sugar, and continue to heat, stirring occasionally, until the sugar is a clear, amber color.

6. Remove from the heat and place the bottom of the pan in the prepared bowl of cold water to stop the cooking.

WORKING WITH CARAMEL

- While caramel is in a liquid state, it can be drizzled with a spoon onto parchment and allowed to harden to create beautiful garnishes.

- When caramel cools enough to be handled but is still warm, it can be hand-pulled into ribbons. For corkscrew embellishments, grease a wooden spoon handle with shortening. Pour the liquid caramel onto a parchment-lined cookie sheet and let it cool slightly. While the candy is still warm and pliable, with a sharp knife, cut long, thin strips, about ¼ inch wide. Pull a caramel strip away from the candy mass and wind it around the spoon. Set the spoon down on the parchment and allow the caramel to set; slide the hardened candy off the spoon handle. Use the caramel corkscrews to garnish ice cream, cake slices, or custards.

- Use hardened caramel immediately.

- Humidity will adversely affect hard caramel, so do not make hard caramel during humid weather and do not store it in the refrigerator.

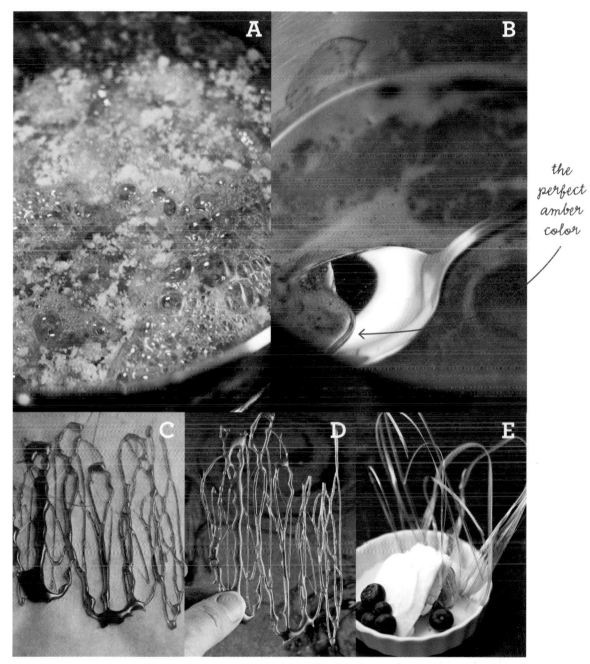

the perfect amber color

A. Bubbling sugar is transformed into caramel. **B.** This amber caramel is ready for use. **C.** Drizzle the liquid caramel onto parchment paper. **D.** Once it hardens, it can be used as a garnish. **E.** Or, when hard caramel has cooled enough to handle, it can be pulled into ribbons.

SPOON DESSERTS

THINGS TO KEEP IN MIND

■ The eggs used in custard and pastry cream require tempering, which means introducing hot liquids very slowly to the eggs. Recipes call for either gradually whisking hot liquid into eggs in a bowl or very slowly pouring beaten eggs in a thin stream directly into hot liquid in a saucepan while whisking constantly. The mixture is then cooked over low heat to thicken it. If you do not use this method, you run the risk of scrambling the eggs and creating a very undesirable texture.

■ Unflavored powdered gelatin is "bloomed" in water before being added to mousse and *panna cotta*. To bloom the gelatin, sprinkle it finely and evenly over liquid as the recipe directs and let stand for 3 to 5 minutes. Avoid dumping the powder in a pile on the liquid's surface; this can cause lumps to form and the gelatin will not be absorbed evenly. When the bloomed gelatin is heated, it becomes a clear liquid and is dissolved evenly for a smooth texture in desserts.

FRUIT MOUSSE

YIELD: Approximately 4 cups

Light, creamy mousse makes a stunning dessert on its own, but it can also be used as a cake filling or as a frozen treat. Use fruit purees with vibrant flavors and colors, such as mango, blackberry, raspberry, or strawberry, but be sure to strain them first to remove any seeds.

---

2 tablespoons unflavored powdered gelatin
¼ cup cold water

2¼ cups loosely packed fresh fruit
¾ cup superfine sugar
1¼ cups heavy cream

---

1. In a small bowl, sprinkle the powdered gelatin over the cold water. Let stand until the gelatin absorbs the water.

2. Microwave for 10 seconds at full power or until the gelatin has melted into a clear liquid. Gelatin can also be melted in a saucepan on the stovetop over medium heat.

3. Place pieces of fruit into a blender or food processor and puree until smooth. If you are using fruit with seeds, such as kiwis or strawberries, strain the puree before proceeding.

4. Combine the fruit puree and sugar; mix well. Pour in the liquid gelatin mixture. Let stand at room temperature until the mixture begins to thicken, about 20 minutes.

5. Whip the heavy cream until stiff peaks form.

6. Stir the fruit puree mixture gently to loosen it. With a large rubber spatula, fold 2 to 3 tablespoons of whipped cream into the fruit puree mixture to relax it.

7. Fold in the remaining cream until blended and there are no longer streaks of fruit visible.

8. Transfer the mousse to serving dishes and chill until ready to serve.

A. Fold a few tablespoons of fruit puree mixture (mango, in this case) into the whipped cream with a rubber spatula before adding the remaining coulis. **B.** When done, fruit mousse should be a consistent color with no white streaks remaining.

VANILLA PASTRY CREAM

YIELD: Approximately 2 cups

When it comes to pastry fillings, it's difficult to top luxurious vanilla pastry cream. Use it to fill sponge cakes, tarts, cream puffs, and éclairs.

2 tablespoons cornstarch
1 cup whole milk
1 egg
2 egg yolks

6 tablespoons sugar
2 tablespoons butter
1 teaspoon vanilla

1. In a small bowl, dissolve the cornstarch in ¼ cup of the milk. Beat the whole egg, then the yolks, one at a time, into the cornstarch mixture.

2. In a saucepan, combine the remaining ¾ cup milk and the sugar; bring to a boil, whisking constantly.

3. While whisking the egg mixture, slowly pour ⅓ of the boiling milk into it, to temper the eggs.

4. Return the remaining milk in the saucepan to medium low heat.

5. Pour the hot egg mixture into the saucepan in a thin stream, whisking, so as to not scramble the eggs.

6. Whisk constantly until the mixture begins to boil. Remove from the heat and whisk in the butter and vanilla.

7. Pour the pastry cream into a bowl and press a sheet of plastic wrap directly on the surface so it does not form a skin. Cool to room temperature.

8. Refrigerate until ready to use.

VARIATIONS

Chocolate Pastry Cream: Stir 3 ounces melted semisweet chocolate into the hot pastry cream.

Coffee Pastry Cream: Stir 2 teaspoons instant espresso powder into the hot pastry cream.

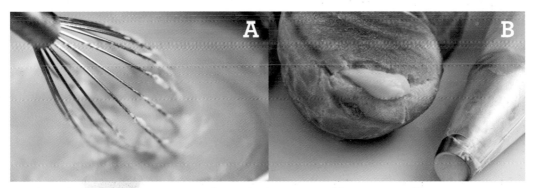

A. Whisk the pastry cream continuously as it heats up to avoid lumps. B. Vanilla pastry cream can be used to fill choux puffs.

CHOCOLATE MOUSSE

YIELD: 5 cups, enough for 6 to 8 servings

Every chocolate lover should have a good recipe for chocolate mousse. This recipe is adapted from Julia Child's *Mousseline au Chocolat* recipe. It is incredibly rich and sure to satisfy the fiercest chocolate craving. If you are serving children or anyone sensitive to caffeine, substitute low-fat chocolate milk for the coffee. This is best enjoyed the day it is made and can be refrigerated for up to 4 hours before serving.

6 ounces semisweet chocolate, chopped
¼ cup strong brewed coffee or espresso
¼ pound plus 4 tablespoons (1½ sticks) butter, cubed
4 eggs, separated
⅔ cup sugar
Pinch of salt
1 teaspoon vanilla extract

1. Fill a large bowl half full of cold water and ice cubes; set aside.

2. Fill a medium saucepan one-third full of water and set over medium-high heat. Bring to a simmer.

3. Combine the chocolate and coffee in a heatproof bowl and place over the saucepan of simmering water. Whisk until smooth. Remove from the heat. Add the butter cubes a few at a time, whisking until the butter is melted and the mixture is smooth; set aside to cool.

4. In a large heatproof bowl, whisk the egg yolks and ⅓ cup of the sugar until thick and pale.

5. Place the bowl over the simmering water and whisk again for 3 to 4 minutes. This can be done by hand or you can use a handheld electric mixer. The mixture will be hot and foamy.

6. Place the yolk-sugar mixture in the bowl of icy water and continue to whisk for 4 minutes,

until the mixture has cooled and forms a thick ribbon on top of the batter when the whisk is lifted from the bowl.

7. Fold the chocolate mixture into the yolk-sugar mixture.

8. In a separate bowl, with an electric mixer, beat the egg whites with the salt until soft peaks form. Gradually beat in the remaining ⅓ cup sugar a little at a time until the whites are thick and shiny.

9. Add the vanilla to the whipped egg whites and beat until well incorporated.

10. Fold a little of the beaten egg whites into the chocolate mixture to loosen it.

11. Using a rubber spatula, carefully fold in the rest of the egg whites just until combined. Do this very gently, so as to not deflate the chocolate mousse.

12. Transfer the mousse to a 5-cup serving dish or divide the mousse among 6 small dessert cups. Chill until ready to serve.

keep it cool!

A. Use the best quality chocolate you can find—this is Green & Black's organic. **B.** Use an ice bath to cool the hot yolk mixture. **C.** Whisk the egg yoke mixture over ice until it is cool and thick.

CRÈME CHANTILLY

YIELD: 2 cups

Most any dessert can be heightened by adding a dollop or two of sweetened whipped cream. Use this classic recipe as a filling for cakes and pastries.

1 cup heavy cream
2 tablespoons superfine sugar
¼ teaspoon pure vanilla extract

1. Pour the heavy cream into a large mixing bowl.

2. Whip the heavy cream with an electric hand mixer until it starts to thicken.

3. Add the sugar and vanilla extract.

4. Whip until stiff peaks form.

5. Use immediately or store in the refrigerator until ready for use.

DIAGONAL CHOCOLATE MOUSSE CUPS

YIELD: 10 servings

In this high-contrast, elegant presentation, chocolate mousse is served in punch cups alongside *Crème Chantilly*.

DESSERT COMPONENTS
2½ cups Chocolate Mousse (see page 60)
2 cups *Crème Chantilly* (see this page)
Chocolate sprinkles, chocolate curls, or crushed chocolate wafers for garnish (optional)

EQUIPMENT
Small clear glass or plastic cups, about 6 ounces each
3 or 4 empty pressed-foam or cardboard egg cartons

1. Place 3 or 4 cups into the cavities of the egg crates. Tilt the cups at a 45-degree angle.

2. Pour in the chocolate mousse, dividing equally among the cups.

3. Refrigerate until the mousse is firm.

4. Place the cups upright (the mousse will remain at an angle) and spoon or pipe in the *Crème Chantilly*, dividing equally among the cups.

5. Garnish as desired.

6. Refrigerate until ready for use, or serve immediately.

Note: The footed punch cups used here measure 3½ inches tall and hold about ¾ cup.

LEMON CURD

YIELD: About 2 cups

Lemon curd should be renamed "sunshine in a bowl." It has a naturally sunny color and a bright, citrusy flavor, which make it a feast for the eyes and the taste buds! Since it is created from very simple pantry staples, it can be made easily and enjoyed often.

¼ pound (1 stick) butter, softened
1 cup sugar
2 eggs, at room temperature
2 egg yolks, at room temperature
⅓ cup plus 4 tablespoons fresh lemon juice

1. Beat the butter and sugar in a large bowl using an electric mixer.

2. Slowly add the eggs and yolks one at a time, mixing well after each addition.

3. Pour in the lemon juice and mix again. Expect the mixture to look curdled; this is normal.

4. Transfer the mixture to a medium saucepan and clip a candy thermometer to the side. Cook over medium heat, stirring constantly, until smooth and no longer curdled.

5. Increase the heat slightly and cook, whisking constantly, until the mixture thickens.

6. Cook, stirring frequently, until the mixture reaches 170°F.

7. Remove the curd from the heat source.

8. Transfer the mixture to a bowl and press plastic wrap on the surface of the lemon curd to keep a skin from forming. Cool to room temperature.

9. Chill the curd in the refrigerator; it will thicken further as it cools.

Note: Covered tightly, lemon curd will keep in the refrigerator for 1 week and in the freezer for 2 months.

VARIATION

Lime Curd: Replace the lemon juice with lime juice.

PANNA COTTA

YIELD: 8 (½-cup) servings

Panna cotta is such an easy and impressive treat to make. Surround it with a sweet berry coulis for a truly special dessert. The mixture can be used to fill shaped molds and inverted onto serving plates, or simply poured into small serving dishes or glasses, chilled, and served with a spoon.

---

1 envelope unflavored powdered gelatin (about 1 tablespoon)	1 cup half-and-half
2 tablespoons cold water	⅓ cup sugar
2 cups heavy cream	1½ teaspoons vanilla extract

---

1. If inverting the *panna cotta*, grease 8 (½-cup) molds or ramekins lightly.

2. In a small saucepan, sprinkle the powdered gelatin over the cold water and let stand until absorbed.

3. Heat the gelatin mixture over low heat for approximately 2 to 3 minutes, or until the gelatin has dissolved. Remove from the heat source.

4. Combine the heavy cream, half-and-half, and sugar in a large saucepan.

5. Heat the mixture until just boiling. Remove from the heat and stir in the melted gelatin mixture.

6. Add the vanilla extract and stir well.

7. Divide the mixture among 8 buttered dessert molds or ramekins.

8. Cover in plastic wrap and let chill in the refrigerator for 4 hours.

9. When set, to unmold, run a thin offset spatula along the edge of each mold or ramekin, and turn the *panna cotta* out onto a small dessert plate.

Note: If the *panna cotta* will not unmold easily, dip the bottoms of the molds in warm water for a few seconds and then invert onto a dessert plate.

VARIATION

Cooonut *Panna Cotta*: Replace the half-and-half with coconut milk and add 2 teaspoons coconut extract.

ICINGS

THINGS TO KEEP IN MIND

■ Before frosting a cake, make sure it is completely cool, and brush away any loose crumbs on the surface with a pastry brush.

■ When assembling and icing cakes, use 4 strips of wax paper to line the cake platter—don't cover the entire surface of the plate with wax paper, just the edges. Center the cake on the serving platter directly on top of the strips and frost it. The wax paper will catch any drips or messy smears during frosting. Gently tug on the wax strips and pull them away from the cake, revealing a clean platter.

■ When a frosting recipe indicates an ingredient amount range (example: 2 to 4 cups confectioners' sugar or 2 to 3 tablespoons liquid) use the smallest amount first and mix thoroughly. Then you can add more sugar or liquid until the desired thickness is reached. This gives you more control over the consistency.

■ If the frosting seems too thick or tears the cake when being applied, thin the mixture with cream or water until it spreads easily.

PIPING BASICS

Piping icing is a tricky procedure that depends on many factors, from the type and consistency of the icing to the size of the tips used. What follows are some basic tips and guidelines that will demystify what for many home bakers can be a daunting process and show you how much fun you can have when you master it.

PIPING BAGS

It is great having cloth piping bags in your equipment drawer, but many other kitchen staples can be used in a pinch—I've even used plastic shopping bags (hole-free and thoroughly cleaned and dried)!

- Cloth piping bags are reusable, economical, and perfect for small decorating jobs, especially when you are dealing with only one or two kinds of icing.

- Clear disposable zip-top bags are ideal when you're working on a large project or with many colors. Though they are not as environmentally friendly, they make it easy to quickly spot the color you need when time is of the essence.

- Rubber bands are great for tying off piping bags and can be reused. Plastic zip ties and twist ties are also handy closures, and most people have a surplus of the latter type rattling around in their junk drawers.

PIPING TIPS

You'll find an endless variety of piping tips at your local craft store. Some create three-dimensional shapes such as ruffles, leaves, and stars. For the royal icing applications in this book, you'll just need a few small round tips in sizes 3 to 5, but it's always fun to have a lot of tips to choose from.

- *Size 3 round*—This is a frequently used tip for stiff-peak and soft-peak icings. This size is ideal for outlining designs to be filled with flood icing. It can also be used for finishing touches on top of dry or set icing, such as dots and swirls.

- *Size 4 round*—This is the most versatile tip. This size can be used for outlining, flooding, and drawing. This is a good "try-out" tip, if you are new to piping and flooding.

- *Size 5 round*—This tip should be used for flooding cookies. It has a large opening, which allows for quick execution, and is great for filling in large areas. Because of the large opening, you have less control over the icing, so this tip is not ideal for drawing, writing, or outlining.

ATTACHING A PIPING TIP TO A PIPING BAG

This is a simple procedure, but should be done carefully every time—nothing's worse than ruining a project due to a leaky piping tip!

- First, place a coupler inside the piping bag, and snip the tip of the piping bag with a pair of scissors.

- Next, press the coupler snugly into the tip of the bag; there should be no plastic overhang, or the tip can clog.

- Finally, place the piping tip over the coupler while keeping a little tension in the pastry bag and screw on the coupler ring.

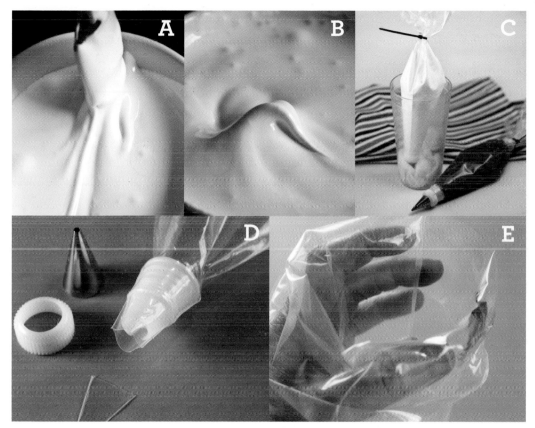

A. The "line" test will tell you when you have the right consistency in a flood icing. **B.** A soft peak icing will fall onto itself. **C.** The bag of white frosting is resting tip down on a damp paper towel to keep the tip from drying or clogging. **D.** Piping essentials: piping bag with coupler, ring, and piping tip. **E.** To avoid icing smears on the outside of the piping bag, fold the sides of the bag down before filling it.

FILLING A PIPING BAG

Filling a piping bag is a straightforward process, but always make sure that you have as few air pockets in the icing in the bag as possible. These pockets of air will cause the icing to splutter out of the bag as you apply it.

When you are using Royal Icing (see pages 70–71), keep in mind that, depending on the consistency of the icing, different methods of filling the piping bag apply:

- *Stiff-peak icing:* Fold one-third of the piping bag down from the top opening. Scoop stiff-peak royal icing into the bag with a large offset spatula. Close the bag and use.

- *Soft-peak or flood icing:* Fold one-third of the piping bag down from the top opening. Place the piping bag in a tall tumbler with a damp paper towel in the bottom, and pour in the icing. While working on a decorating project using either of these consistencies, keep bags of icing in tall tumblers with a damp paper towel at the bottom. The towel keeps the icing from drying in, or running out of, the tip.

ROYAL ICING

Royal icing is simplicity itself, made from egg whites and confectioners' sugar. It is also versatile and does a great many jobs in the confectionery world. In this book, we will be working with three consistencies: stiff peak, soft peak, and flood.

- *Stiff-peak icing* dries to a smooth, hard, candy-like finish. It is used to create intricate latticework and such decorative flourishes as candy flowers. It is also the edible mortar that holds gingerbread houses together. Stiff-peak icing requires no thinning with water.

- *Soft-peak icing* is looser than stiff-peak icing. It easily flows through very small piping tips and is ideal for outlining and drawing on cookies. To achieve it, add a few drops of water at a time to stiff-peak icing, folding until it is the desired consistency. You've reached soft-peak consistency when a spoon dipped in and pulled from the icing forms a peak that falls onto itself.

- *Flood icing* has a very thin consistency and dries to a smooth, satiny finish. It is used to fill in shapes made with soft-peak or stiff-peak royal icing. Flood icing is bit trickier to achieve. Fold in a few drops of water at a time to soft-peak icing; as you fold, check the consistency by dragging a spoon through the center of the mixture in a straight line, creating an indentation. When the icing is of perfect flood consistency, the indentation should completely disappear in 10 seconds. If it disappears too quickly, then your icing is too thin and will not dry properly. (This is especially problematic when decorating cookies; the flood icing will run outside stiff-peak or soft-peak outlines.) The indentation should disappear as close to the 10-second mark as possible. It is much harder to thicken the icing after it has been thinned than it is to make thick icing thinner, so take your time and add water drops a few at a time. If your icing does get too runny, you can add sifted confectioners' sugar a little at a time until the desired consistency is achieved.

Note: Gel food colorings are ideal for tinting royal icings because they are concentrated and have less water content than liquid food colorings. Mix gel in a little at a time to achieve the desired color.

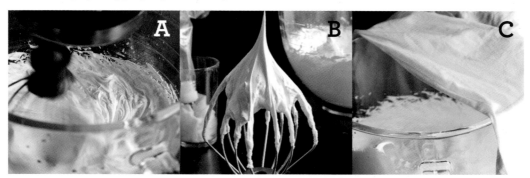

A. For stiff-peak icing, beat the icing until it is thick and fluffy. **B.** A stiff peak royal icing will make a point that stands on its own. **C.** Cover unused icing with a wet towel to avoid crusting.

ROYAL ICING WITH MERINGUE POWDER

YIELD: Approximately 3 cups of icing

This recipe makes stiff-peak icing. To make soft-peak or flood icing, add water to achieve the desired consistency by following the instructions opposite.

---

4 cups confectioners' sugar, sifted
3 tablespoons meringue powder
½ cup warm water, plus more for thinning to soft-peak or flood consistency
½ teaspoon clear flavoring extract (lemon, orange, almond, clear vanilla)
Gel food coloring

---

1. In the bowl of an electric mixer fitted with the whisk attachment, stir the confectioners' sugar and meringue powder on low speed until combined.

2. Add the water and beat on medium high speed until very stiff peaks form, 5 to 7 minutes.

3. Add the flavoring and beat on low until combined; divide and tint as necessary, using gel food coloring. Bring to desired consistency by whisking in additional drops of water.

4. Use the icing immediately or drape a damp tea towel over the mixing bowl or bowls to prevent the icing from drying out.

Note: Royal icing should be used immediately or transferred to airtight containers and refrigerated. Bring to room temperature and stir before using.

ROYAL ICING WITH EGG WHITES

YIELD: Approximately 3 cups of icing

This recipe makes stiff-peak icing. To make soft-peak or flood icing, follow the instructions opposite. Before you make this icing, keep in mind that pregnant women and individuals with compromised immune systems should not consume eggs that are not fully cooked.

---

2 egg whites
2 teaspoons fresh lemon juice
3 cups confectioners' sugar, sifted
Warm water, for thinning to soft peak or flood consistency
½ teaspoon lemon, clear vanilla, or almond flavoring
Gel food coloring

---

1. In the bowl of an electric mixer fitted with the whisk attachment, beat the egg whites with the lemon juice until combined.

2. Add the sifted confectioners' sugar and beat on low speed until combined and smooth. Add desired flavoring and mix until well incorporated. Divide as necessary and tint portions as desired.

3. Bring to desired consistency with warm water and use immediately or drape a damp towel over the bowl.

CHOCOLATE GANACHE

YIELD: About 1½ cups liquid ganache, or, when whipped, enough to ice a 9-inch, 3-layer cake

This ganache is fantastic both in flavor and in versatility. Use it as a decadent fruit dip or a glossy cake glaze. Whip it up with an electric mixer for a fluffy frosting or cake filling.

9 ounces semisweet or bittersweet chocolate
1 cup heavy cream

1. Roughly chop the chocolate and place it in a medium bowl.

2. In a small saucepan, heat the heavy cream over medium-high heat until just boiling.

3. Pour the hot cream over the chocolate and whisk until the chocolate is melted and the mixture is smooth.

4. Allow to cool slightly before using as a glaze or dip.

Note: For a thick, fluffy icing, pour the cooled ganache into the bowl of a mixer and beat on high with the whisk attachment for 5 minutes.

smooth and fluffy!

A. Before it is whipped, chocolate ganache can be used as a glossy cake topping. Then whip the rest and apply it as fluffy frosting to the sides of the cake. **B.** Freshly whipped Swiss Buttercream.

SWISS BUTTERCREAM

YIELD: 4½ cups icing, enough for a 9-inch, 3-layer cake

Swiss meringue buttercream is a silky-smooth icing that is made with egg whites and hot sugar syrup. Heralded by pastry chefs and home cooks alike, it pipes beautifully and remains extremely stable at room temperature. For this reason, it is ideal for wedding cakes and other celebration cakes of great importance.

5 egg whites
1 cup sugar
Pinch of salt
1 pound (4 sticks) butter, cubed, at room temperature
2 teaspoons clear vanilla extract

1. Set a saucepan filled one-third full of water over medium-high heat and bring to a simmer.

2. Whisk together the egg whites, sugar, and salt in a large heatproof bowl. Set over the simmering water and whisk until the mixture is hot to the touch and the sugar has dissolved.

3. Transfer the mixture to the bowl of a stand mixer fitted with the whisk attachment.

4. Beat on low speed for 2 minutes. Increase to medium-high until stiff peaks are formed.

5. Continue beating at medium-high speed until the mixture is fluffy and has cooled (the mixing bowl should feel cool to the touch).

6. Turn the mixer off and switch from the whisk attachment to the paddle. Turn the mixer on medium-low and add the butter, a few cubes at a time, beating until well incorporated before the next addition.

7. Add the vanilla extract.

8. Beat until the frosting is thick and completely smooth.

9. Store in an airtight container until ready for use. Swiss buttercream can be chilled in the refrigerator for up to 3 days or frozen for up to 3 months. To use, bring to room temperature and rewhip in the stand mixer with the paddle until fluffy and smooth.

VARIATIONS

Chocolate Swiss Buttercream: Gently melt 5 ounces semisweet chocolate and let cool. Fold into the finished buttercream with a rubber spatula.

Citrus-Flavored Swiss Buttercream: Use orange, lemon, or lime oil, or a combination, to flavor the buttercream to taste.

Nut-Flavored Swiss Buttercream: Use nut flavoring oils (hazelnut, almond, or another of your choice) to flavor the buttercream to taste.

FONDANT AND PIPING GEL

YIELD: Approximately 1 pound fondant; 2 cups piping gel

Rolled fondant is used to create flawlessly smooth cake coverings. For those not experienced with fondant, I suggest you use the ready-made variety that is sold in cake-decorating supply stores. It is firm but pliable and holds its shape when it dries.

Once you get a feel for the ready-made fondant's texture and become comfortable using it to cover cakes, try making your own from this recipe. This recipe calls for liquid glucose, which can be purchased at cake supply shops or craft stores such as JoAnn's, Michael's, and AC Moore.

Piping gel is an integral part of holding together decorative fondant pieces and coverings. It is a better adhesive than plain corn syrup.

FONDANT

    1 egg white, or egg white powder
        (albumen) equal to 1 egg according
        to manufacturer's instructions on
        package
    2 tablespoons liquid glucose
    4½ cups confectioners' sugar, sifted,
        plus more for kneading
    White vegetable shortening (optional)

PIPING GEL

    2 tablespoons unflavored powdered
        gelatin
    2 tablespoons cold water
    2 cups light corn syrup

Make the fondant:

1. In a large bowl, combine the egg white and liquid glucose.

2. Sift the confectioners' sugar (again!) into the bowl approximately 1 cup at a time. Stir well after each addition.

3. When the mixture is too thick to stir, knead it with your fingers. Turn the fondant out onto a work surface that has been generously dusted with confectioners' sugar.

4. Knead the fondant until it is soft and pliable. Roll it out as desired. If the fondant is too dry and cracks or tears, knead in a little vegetable shortening. If it is too sticky, knead in a little more confectioners' sugar.

5. Use immediately, store in a zip-top bag with the air removed, or double-wrap in plastic wrap.

Amount of fondant you will need for a double layer cake:

5-inch square, 6-inch round	1 pound
7-inch square, 8-inch round	1¾ pounds
8-inch square, 9-inch round	2 pounds
9-inch square, 10-inch round	2½ pounds
10-inch square, 11-inch round	3¾ pounds
11-inch square, 12-inch round	4 pounds

A. Stir confectioners' sugar into the egg whites and glucose a little at a time. **B.** Stir the mixture well until a white paste forms. **C.** Once the mixture is too thick to stir, knead it right in the bowl. **D.** Fondant, ready to be rolled!

Make the piping gel:

1. Sprinkle the gelatin over the water in a small saucepan. Let stand until absorbed.

2. Place the saucepan over low heat and cook until the mixture is clear and the gelatin has dissolved. Do not boil.

3. Stir in the corn syrup and increase heat to medium-low. Cook just until very hot but not boiling.

4. Remove from heat and cool completely before use.

Note: Will keep for 2 months refrigerated in a sealed container.

Coat cake layers in fondant:

1. First, level the cake layers, with either a serrated knife or a cake leveler.

2. Brush the cake with flavored simple syrup and fill it with the desired filling (if using). Apply a thin layer of American buttercream (see page 80), called the crumb coat, to the cake to glue down any loose crumbs. Let this layer stand at room temperature until a crust forms.

3. Using plastic gloves to avoid staining your hands, tint the fondant by kneading in a little gel food coloring, if desired.

4. Lightly dust a work surface with confectioners' sugar. With a fondant roller, roll out the fondant to a ¼-inch thickness, picking it up and turning it often as you roll it flat. Dust the work surface with confectioners' sugar intermittently if the fondant sticks.

Note: Ready-made fondant requires kneading before it can be rolled.

5. Drape the rolled fondant over a rolling pin and lift it onto the cake.

6. Gently flatten the fondant on the top of the cake with a fondant smoother. Pick up one side of the fondant overhang at the bottom edge of the cake. Smooth the fondant down onto the cake side with your hand. Continue to smooth the fondant down around the sides of the cake until it is fitted firmly against the cake. This will take a few minutes of working. When the fondant is crease-free on all sides, use the fondant smoother to work out any uneven spots.

Note: Do not stretch or pull the fondant downward.

7. With a plain-edge knife, trim off the extra fondant, leaving about 2 inches of excess around the edge. This small amount of fondant can be more precisely trimmed off than a large overhang of fondant.

8. Trim the remaining small amount of fondant from the bottom edge of the cake with a sharp plain-edge knife or a pizza cutter. Fondant-covered cakes can be stored at room temperature for up to 2 days. It is not recommended to refrigerate fondant-covered cakes, but if the filling requires refrigeration, the cake can be covered in plastic wrap and refrigerated overnight. When refrigerated fondant-covered cakes are brought to room temperature, sweating can occur. The beads of condensed water that may form on the warming fondant should not be touched or the fondant will be damaged. Allow water to evaporate over time.

E. Cover the cake in a buttercream crumb-coat to ready it to be covered in fondant. F. A fondant roller has a smooth surface to make the fondant flawless when rolled out. G. Excess fondant needs to be trimmed from the cake. H. A fondant-covered cake—the perfect blank canvas for a baker.

MARZIPAN

YIELD: About 1 pound

Marzipan is made primarily of almond meal and sugar. It is used as a cake covering and applied in the same fashion as rolled fondant. Decorative flourishes such as hand-modeled fruits and Christmas candies are traditionally made from this versatile confection.

2¼ cups blanched, ground almonds or prepackaged almond flour
1 cup confectioners' sugar
½ cup superfine sugar
1 teaspoon lemon juice
2 drops almond extract
1 egg, beaten

1. In the bowl of a large stand mixer fitted with the paddle attachment, stir together the ground almonds, confectioners' sugar, and superfine sugar.

2. Add the lemon juice and almond extract; stir again.

3. Exchange the paddle attachment for the dough hook.

4. Turn the mixer on low and slowly pour the beaten egg into the almond mixture.

5. The mixture will begin to clump and form a paste.

6. Continue to knead with the dough hook until smooth.

7. Turn the dough out onto a piece of wax paper and roll into a log. Use immediately, wrap tightly in wax paper and store in a zip-top bag with the air removed, or wrap tightly in two layers of plastic wrap. Store marzipan in the refrigerator; bring to room temperature before using.

Note: When covering a cake in marzipan, first apply flavored simple syrup or melted jam with a pastry brush to the surface of the cake to help the marzipan adhere. Marzipan will harden and become unusable if not stored properly.

A. Use the paddle attachment to mix the dry ingredients. B. Use the dough hook to mix wet ingredients into dry ones. C. With the mixer on, slowly add wet ingredients to the dry ones. D. The marzipan dough will begin to form clumps. E. The dough is properly mixed when it forms a ball. F. One pound of fresh marzipan.

AMERICAN BUTTERCREAM

YIELD: 2 cups

American buttercream is one of the easiest and quickest frostings you can make. It is well-known as a birthday-cake covering and can be assembled using only 3 ingredients: butter, confectioners' sugar, and vanilla. It is easily adapted by adding your choice of colorings and flavorings.

The natural color of this buttercream is ivory. Pristine white can be achieved by replacing half of the butter with vegetable shortening and by using a clear flavoring or extract. Specialty whitening additives are sold in cake supply stores.

½ pound (2 sticks) butter, softened
2½ cups confectioners' sugar
1 teaspoon vanilla extract
Milk or heavy cream, if necessary

1. In a stand mixer fitted with the whisk attachment, mix together the butter and confectioners' sugar. Begin mixing on low speed until the mixture is crumbly. Increase to high and beat for 3 minutes.

2. Add the vanilla extract and beat again for another minute until light and fluffy.

Note: If you find that the buttercream is too stiff, you may add milk or heavy cream 1 tablespoon at a time until the mixture is of spreading consistency.

TIP

Start the mixer at low speed; this will help incorporate the ingredients without covering your entire kitchen (and you) in a cloud of confectioners' sugar.

VARIATIONS

Chocolate Buttercream: Add ¼ cup of sifted unsweetened cocoa powder to the confectioners' sugar.

Citrus Buttercream: Replace the vanilla extract with orange, lemon, or lime extract plus 1 teaspoon citrus zest.

Coffee Buttercream: Add instant espresso powder to desired strength. Start with 1½ teaspoons espresso and increase by ½-teaspoon amount to achieve a stronger coffee flavor

PASTRIES AND CRUSTS

THINGS TO KEEP IN MIND

▦ When making tart and *pâte sablée* crust, make sure the butter is cold. Pieces of cold butter create pockets of steam while the dough bakes, which results in a flaky, tender crust. If the butter is too soft when worked into dry ingredients, it will essentially melt and begin to absorb flour before it is baked, which can make the crust tough. To be thoroughly chilled, refrigerated butter may be placed in the freezer for a few minutes before using.

▦ Tart crust dough is very tender. If it separates or tears while being pressed into the pan, pinch the dough back together or use a small scrap of dough to mend the tear.

▦ When making *pâte à choux*, be sure to keep the oven door closed until the puffs or éclairs are golden brown. Opening the door may cause the pastry puffs to deflate

PÂTE À CHOUX

YIELD: 30 cream puff shells, or 12 éclair shells

The way choux puffs bake into a perfectly hollow shell is magical. "Pot-ah-shoe," as it is pronounced, is a thick flour paste that is lightened with whole eggs and used for cream puffs, éclairs, and profiteroles. Cheese can be added, or the puffs can be filled with savory fillings and served as an appetizer for a party. I'm always delighted when I split one open to find the perfect hollow pocket for a generous amount of filling. This recipe can also be used to make éclair shells.

¾ cup water
6 tablespoons butter
1 tablespoon sugar
¼ teaspoon salt

1 cup all-purpose flour
4 eggs
Egg wash: 1 egg, lightly beaten with a
    pinch of salt

---

1. Line two baking sheets with parchment paper. Fit a pastry bag with a large plain round tip (or snip ½ inch off the tip of a filled disposable pastry bag).

2. In a medium saucepan, combine the water, butter, sugar, and salt and set over medium heat. Bring to a boil, stirring occasionally.

3. When the mixture reaches a boil, remove the saucepan from the heat source and sift in the flour. Stir to combine.

4. Return the saucepan to the heat and cook while stirring constantly until the dough begins to pull away from the sides of the saucepan.

5. Transfer the dough to a bowl and stir for 1 to 2 minutes to cool slightly. Preheat the oven to 425°F.

6. Add 1 of the eggs to the bowl. As you mix, the dough will break into pieces and appear loose and shiny. As the egg becomes incorporated, the dough will become coarse looking, like mashed potatoes. When this happens, add another egg and repeat the process until you have incorporated all the eggs.

7. Transfer the dough to the pastry bag. Pipe the dough into mounds that are 1 inch long and 1 inch wide, spaced 1½ inches apart on the lined baking sheets.

8. Using a clean finger dipped in water, gently press down on any peaks that have formed during piping. Choux puffs should have rounded tops.

9. Brush the tops with the egg wash.

10. Bake for 10 to 12 minutes, or until the choux puffs are well-inflated and golden.

11. Lower the oven temperature to 350°F and continue to bake the choux until dry, about 20 minutes more.

12. Transfer the choux puffs to a wire rack and let cool.

13. To fill the choux, pierce the side of each puff with a knife, making a small incision just big enough to fit a pastry tip inside. Pipe in desired filling and press gently to close incision.

looks like mashed potatoes!

A. When the first stage of dough is done, it will pull away from the pan and form a ball. **B.** Add the eggs one at a time. **C.** When the eggs are fully incorporated, the dough will lose its gloss. **D.** After piping dollops of dough, dip your finger in water, then flatten the peaks. **E.** Choux puffs ready for the oven. **F.** These golden brown choux puffs are begging to be filled.

ÉCLAIR SHELLS

To make éclair shells, pipe the dough into twelve fingers (approximately 4 inches long) spaced 1½ inches apart on the lined baking sheets, and bake as the recipe indicates.

When the shells have cooled completely, slice in half lengthwise. You will need about 2 cups of filling to fill the éclair shells.

PÂTE SABLÉE

YIELD: 1 (8-inch) tart or about 15 (2-inch) cookies

Pâte sablée is a classic French pastry dough that can be used as a tart crust or rolled and cut into cookies.

1½ cup plus 2 tablespoons all-purpose
   flour, plus more for rolling
1 teaspoon baking powder
7 tablespoons butter, ice cold and
   cubed

⅓ teaspoon salt
2 egg yolks, at room temperature
6 tablespoons plus 1 teaspoon sugar
1 teaspoon vanilla extract

1. In the bowl of a food processor, combine the flour, baking powder, butter, and salt. Pulse until the mixture resembles coarse, pea-size crumbs.

2. In a separate bowl, whisk the egg yolks, sugar, and vanilla extract until lightened in color.

3. Pour the egg mixture in the food processor.

4. Pulse in short bursts until the dough just comes together. If you find that the dough is still a little too crumbly to come together, add a few drops of water and process again, until the dough forms a ball.

5. Turn the dough out onto a piece of wax paper.

6. Shape into a disc and cover with plastic wrap.

7. Leave to rest in the fridge for 30 minutes.

8. Preheat the oven to 375°F. If you are making cookies, line 2 sheet pans with parchment paper. If you are making a tart, lightly grease tart pan with shortening.

9. On a floured work surface, roll the dough into a circle about ¼ inch thick.

10. For an 8-inch tart, press the dough into a tart pan. For cookies, cut into shapes with cutters.

11. For a tart with filling that needs to be baked, lightly grease the tart pan with shortening and par-bake the shell until set, about 7 minutes, before adding the filling and baking again until set and golden. If you are filling the tart with lemon curd or pastry cream, bake the shell until light golden brown, about 20 minutes. Cookies should be baked until the edges are beginning to turn golden, 15 to 18 minutes.

USES FOR *PÂTE SABLÉE* TART SHELLS

This shell can be used instead of piecrust for fillings such as pecan, pumpkin, or lemon. Simply bake the shell until set, about 7 minutes, remove from the oven, fill with your choice of filling, and bake again until set and crust is golden brown (baking times will vary somewhat, depending on filling).

It can also be baked completely, allowed to cool, and filled with vanilla pastry cream or lemon curd.

COOKIE CRUST

YIELD: 1 (9- or 10-inch) crust or 6 (3-inch) individual tart crusts

This crust is ideal for refrigerator pies and no-bake cheesecakes. It requires no baking and can be assembled in just minutes. Crushed chocolate and vanilla wafer cookies can be used in place of the graham cracker crumbs.

2½ cups fine graham cracker or cookie crumbs
¼ pound (1 stick) butter, melted
1½ tablespoons sugar
Pinch of salt

1. Combine the ingredients in a large bowl.

2. Mix well, making sure that all the crumbs are well coated with butter.

3. Press evenly into the bottom of an unlined 9- or 10-inch springform pan (it is not necessary to line it with parchment paper). If making individual tarts, place 6 pastry rings on individual sheets of plastic wrap. Divide the crust mixture evenly among them and press tight with a flat-bottomed tumbler.

graham cracker crust

A. A no-bake cheesecake with a cookie-crust bottom and two layers of cheesecake, one tinted red.
B. A baked tart crust.

TART CRUST

YIELD: Approximately 2½ cups, enough for 8 to 10 small apples, 20 crab apples, or ½ pound grapes or cherries

This tart crust is remarkably easy to make and comes out perfectly every time. It takes just a couple of spins in the food processor to have beautiful buttery pastry dough.

---

1 cup all-purpose flour, plus more for kneading
3 tablespoons sugar
½ teaspoon salt
¼ pound (1 stick) cold butter, cut into ½-inch cubes

1 teaspoon grated lemon zest
1 egg yolk
½ teaspoon pure vanilla extract
1 tablespoon water

---

1. Generously grease a tart pan with vegetable shortening.

2. Pulse the flour, sugar, and salt in a food processor until combined.

3. Add the butter and zest and pulse until the mixture resembles coarse meal with some small pea-size butter lumps.

4. Add the egg yolk, vanilla, and water and pulse until just incorporated and the dough begins to form large clumps.

5. Turn out the dough on a lightly floured surface and knead slightly. Gather the dough together and form into a ball. Flatten into a disc or rectangle, depending on what shape pan you are using.

6. Press the dough over the bottom and up the sides of the pan in an even layer with well floured fingers. Chill the shell for 45 minutes.

7. Preheat the oven to 375°F.

8. Lightly prick the bottom of the shell many times with a fork, and bake until the sides are set and the edge is golden, about 20 minutes.

9. Cool the shell completely in the pan on a rack.

SUGGESTIONS FOR TART SHELL USE

- **Chocolate Tart:** Fill the baked, cooled tart shell with cooled liquid chocolate ganache. Refrigerate until set and serve with fresh whipped cream and raspberries.

- **Lemon Blueberry Tart:** Fill the baked, cooled tart shell with freshly made lemon curd. Refrigerate until set. Top with fresh blueberries and dust with confectioners' sugar before serving.

- **Tropical Fruit Tart:** Fill the baked, cooled tart shell with vanilla pastry cream. Top with slices of kiwi, pineapple, and mango and sprinkle with toasted coconut.

LINE

Easy painting and drawing techniques can make confectionery treats look extra special. In this section you'll learn how to draw mehndi-inspired designs onto gingerbread hands and how to make cookies inspired by textiles and prints. You'll also learn how to create templates and make your own culinary paints to create your own edible art.

CULINARY PAINTS

Amidst some very fun experimentation and studies of food-safe hues, I've found that culinary pigments go far beyond the grocery-store box of food-coloring squeeze tubes. Although that same reliable pantry staple is great for tinting batters and icings, the colorings described in this section are best applied with an artist's brush.

From left to right: Matcha green tea powder, red powdered food coloring, espresso powder, dark cocoa powder.

CRUSHED PIGMENTS

Naturally occurring hues can be derived from food powders. Some of these are common baking staples that you may already have in your pantry. Cocoa powder, espresso powder, and matcha tea powder are all examples of culinary crushed pigments. A wetting agent such as hot water, alcohol-based extracts, or vodka will create a fine-bodied paint that can be used for artistic application on cookies and fondants. When using food-derived paints, you should always be mindful of the flavor pairing. Sepia-toned espresso paint is beautiful and delicious on coffee-flavored *macarons*; however, you may want to refrain from using it on lemon shortbread.

Powdered food colorings are an alternative to natural confectioners' hues. They are available at specialty baking shops and online in a wide array of colors. These flavorless powders can be made into paint in the same manner as natural food powders; however, they are ultra concentrated and should be used with care. They may stain clothes, the hands, or the mouth. Used with vodka as the wetting agent, coloring powders are vibrant and the application is smooth. They are also useful in culinary applications that prohibit the use of water, such as tinting chocolate or sugars.

Mixing Crushed Pigments

Small condiment cups or compartmented paint palettes are ideal for mixing hues.
Begin by using 1 part powder to 1 part wetting agent. Here, I've used ½ teaspoon matcha powder with ½ teaspoon clear almond extract. Stir the mixture using a sturdy flat-head

A. From top to bottom: Matcha tea powder dissolved in almond extract; espresso powder dissolved in vodka; cocoa powder dissolved in hot water. **B.** Mixing matcha tea paint with a brush.

paintbrush. Increase the amount of wetting agent until the desired consistency is reached.

Note: Also try other natural pigments such as beet and carrot powder.

Tips:

• When using natural powders such as matcha or unsweetened cocoa, be careful to not mix paint too thickly. It will clump on top of the confection and taste bitter.

• Designate a test piece of fondant or cookie to gauge the behavior of your mixed paint. You may need to thicken it with extra pigment or thin it with a few drops of wetting agent depending on the confection's surface.

• If a powder does not respond well to alcohol as a wetting agent, try using hot water.

• Corn syrup can be added to the paint mixture to create more body (or thickness) for a textured application.

• The alcohol in mixed powder paint evaporates quickly and thickens the mixture if left sitting out for too long. Additional drops of alcohol may be used to bring the paint back to the desired consistency.

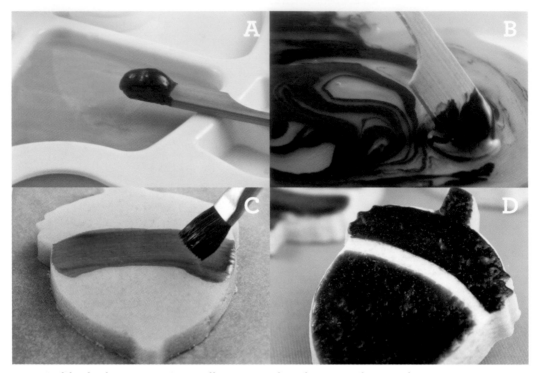

A. Use gel food coloring to tint egg yolk. B. Stir in the coloring until it is uniform. C. Tempera can be brushed onto canvases like unbaked sugar cookies. D. A baked sugar-cookie acorn with tempera coloring. Baking causes the colors to deepen.

EGG TEMPERA FOR BAKING

I'm borrowing the name tempera as a description for this paint because it reminds me so much of a medium that artists have been using for ages. It was one of the first paints I learned to make myself as a young artist. Essentially, tempera paint is made with a pigment (powder or paste) and an egg yolk, which is used as a binding agent. I have always been amazed by the simplicity of this paint, and I'm not alone in that. Ancient Egyptians used a form of tempera to decorate sarcophagi, and it was used by the old masters and in such paintings as Leonardo da Vinci's *The Last Supper*.

In our application, we'll use egg yolk with gel or powder food coloring instead of artists' pigments. This food-safe tempera is painted onto cutout cookies with an artist's brush before they are baked. This paint is flavorless and has a pretty glossy finish, but it must be baked since it contains raw egg.

This paint is best used on unbaked cutout cookies such as sugar cookies, shortbread, or *pâte sablée*. Bake according to the instructions in the cookie recipe.

You will need:

- 1 egg yolk per pigment
- ½ teaspoon gel or powdered food coloring (more or less to desired strength)

1. Separate the egg yolk from the egg white. Pierce the yolk, and allow the yellow to pour from the outer membrane into a small bowl.

2. Discard the membrane. Mix the gel or powder coloring into the yolk until no yellow streaks remain and a uniform color is achieved. If the paint is too thick, use a few drops of water to thin the mixture.

3. Brush the unbaked cookie surface with the tempera.

GEL FOOD-COLORING PAINTS

Gel food-coloring paints are perhaps the easiest paints to make. They can be used at full strength or diluted with alcohol for a quick-drying finish. The thickness of the paint is determined by the amount of wetting agent.

To get a sense of how easy gel food-coloring paints are to use, try this simple exercise. First, place dots of red, yellow, and blue gel close together in a vertical line. Then, using a brush soaked in water or vodka, place the bristles in the dots of red, yellow, and blue gel. Press the brush downward and pull sideways across a smooth surface, such as white rolled fondant. As the water is released, the brushstroke produces a rainbow. This brush technique is called a *wash*. A wash is a painting technique in which the brush is loaded with solvent and a little paint and then pulled in a continuous stroke across the work surface.

this is called a "wash"

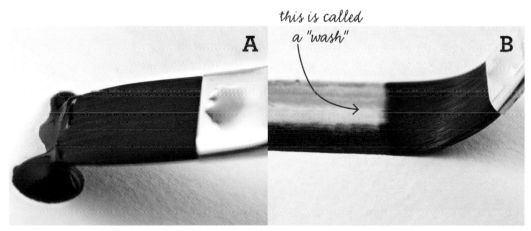

A. Load a brush with water, then dip it in red, yellow, and blue gel food coloring. **B.** A stroke of the damp brush creates a rainbow.

BRUSHES

When choosing paintbrushes for culinary application, purchase soft-haired sable, synthetic, or pony-hair bristles. These are just sturdy enough to provide clean brushstrokes, but still soft enough to protect the surface you are painting on from being damaged. Do not swap paintbrushes with those you use for painting or crafts; keep a separate set that is used for baking and desserts only. Following are examples of brushes I commonly keep with my cake-decorating tools.

- Round number 2
- Round number 5
- Round number 8
- Flat ⅜
- Flat ¾

A sponge dipped in food coloring creates texture.

Natural and synthetic sponges provide an interesting texture to royal icing and fondant surfaces. They can be used dry or moistened for greater color saturation.

Exercise: Brushstrokes

While it's true that different brushes make different lines and shapes, a single brush can also make many types of marks. This exercise uses only one brush, a bit of gel food coloring, and a small amount of rolled fondant as a canvas. Also have available a dish of clear alcohol as a wetting agent for diluting the color and cleaning your brush.

The purpose of this exercise is to become comfortable with the process and gain control of the paintbrush.

Here are some examples of how to use a single brush to make various marks.

Note: The exercise demonstrated is done using a number 5 round paintbrush.

Brushes and their many strokes.

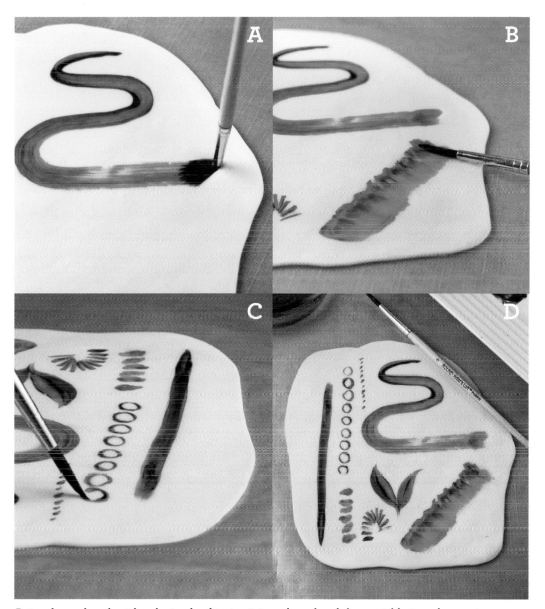

A. Load your brush with coloring by dipping it into the gel and then quickly into the wetting agent. Repeat if necessary. When the brush is loaded with coloring, begin making an S shape, starting with the tip of the brush, gradually increasing pressure, and ending with the hilt. This will give you an idea of the size range your brush has. **B.** Saturate the brush again. This time lay it flat on its side and roll it across the fondant's surface. This technique is sometimes used in landscape painting. **C.** The fine point on this brush can handle tedious detail work. Practice a steady hand by making small circles on the fondant. **D.** Further experiment by making lines, dots, and dashes.

CREATING A TEMPLATE

Drawing and painting can seem intimidating, but those who are concerned about being an "artist" need not worry. Templates make it easy to draw designs and intricate details without the fear of failure.

The fun part is that you can choose almost any image to replicate, including clip art printed from the computer or a design from a book or magazine. Images with bold, simple lines translate best as drawn confectionery. Beginners should choose this type of image for practice.

Tip: Piping a template is much the same as piping royal icing onto a cookie. Hold the tip above the surface and allow the icing to fall evenly on the surface below.

Piping a Template

1. Lay the design on a flat work surface. Cover with a large piece of semitransparent parchment paper. Unbleached parchment works well.

2. Prepare the material you plan to pipe. Royal icing, melted chocolate, melted almond bark, and candy melts are all ideal for piping. Any material that can be piped and dries solid, like chocolate, can be used with this type of template.

3. For small lines, use a piping bag fitted with a small tip (3 or 4 round) or place melted chocolate in a disposable piping bag (or zip-top bag) with the one corner snipped off.

4. Fill the bag no more than half full so it will be comfortable to hold and easier to control than a bag filled to the top. Close the open end with a rubber band if using a piping bag.

5. Hold the bag at a 45-degree angle, with the tip 1 inch above the paper.

6. Pipe the design using steady, controlled pressure, allowing the piping material to fall onto the parchment paper. Do not place the tip directly on the paper (or cookie) and drag it across the surface. Doing so makes a very messy-looking line.

Creating a Template for Gum Paste or Fondant

Images can also be traced onto transparent paper and used to cut out pieces of fondant and gum paste.

1. Tint and roll gum paste or fondant to a ¼-inch thickness.

2. Place your chosen image under a piece of semitransparent paper (copy paper will do nicely) and trace it onto the paper.

3. Lay the paper template over the rolled fondant or paste and cut through both the image and the gum paste with an X-Acto knife.

4. Remove the template and the paper scraps cut from the template.

5. Remove the gum paste from around the cutout image.

6. Smooth slightly with a fondant roller.

7. Apply as a decoration to the side of a cake, or let harden and use as a cake topper.

made using templates, no special talent required

X-Acto knife

A. Chocolate trees created from a template under parchment paper. **B.** A deer template placed over gum paste **C.** Use an X-Acto knife to make clean-cut lines. Be sure to use a new blade for each project. **D.** Smooth the surface of the gum paste with a fondant roller.

MEHNDI HAND COOKIES

YIELD: Approximately 15 hand cookies

A few years ago, my best friend was experiencing some turbulence in her life, so I decided she needed a batch of homemade cookies to make her feel better. I wanted to make something fun and personal, yet artful and representative of good fortune. Ann is a talented artist with an extensive background in printmaking. Early in our friendship, we both were intrigued by the beauty of mehndi design. We even threw a henna party once.

The idea came to me that I should do a mehndi-inspired cookie for her.

3½ cups all-purpose flour
2 teaspoons ground ginger
1½ teaspoons ground cinnamon
1 teaspoon baking soda
½ teaspoon salt
¼ teaspoon ground allspice
¼ teaspoon grated nutmeg

½ pound (2 sticks) butter, at room
    temperature
¾ cup packed dark brown sugar
½ cup molasses (not blackstrap)
1 egg, at room temperature
½ teaspoon vanilla extract

---

1. In a large bowl, sift the flour, ginger, cinnamon, baking soda, salt, allspice, and nutmeg. Set aside.

2. In the bowl of a stand mixer fitted with the paddle attachment, beat the butter at medium speed until smooth.

3. Add the brown sugar and beat for 1 minute.

4. Add the molasses and beat until well combined, about 2 minutes.

5. Add the egg and beat until well blended, about 1 minute.

6. Reduce the mixer speed to low and beat in the vanilla extract.

7. With the mixer still on low speed, beat in the flour mixture until just combined.

8. Turn the dough out onto wax paper and form into a ball; divide the ball in half. Form each half into a ball. Flatten the balls into two discs. Wrap each disc in a double covering of plastic wrap. Chill the dough in the refrigerator for 2 to 4 hours.

9. While waiting for the dough to chill, make a template by tracing your hand on a piece of heavy stock craft paper or a piece of sturdy cardboard. Do not spread your fingers out for tracing; a closed-hand silhouette makes for a larger canvas to draw on.

10. When the dough is chilled, roll out each disc between two sheets of wax paper to a ¼-inch thickness with a rolling pin.

11. Preheat the oven to 350°F. Line two baking sheets with parchment paper.

12. Place the template on top of the dough and cut around it with a plain-edge knife. Repeat until all the dough is used. Cookie-dough scraps can be kneaded and rerolled until all the dough is used.

13. Transfer the hand-shaped cookies to the prepared baking sheets. Using the back of a knife, score the lines between the fingers without cutting completely through the dough.

14. Bake for 8 minutes for child-size hands and 12 to 15 minutes for adult-size hands.

15. Transfer to a wire rack and let cool completely.

EMBELLISHMENT IDEAS

After baking the cookies, you're ready for embellishment.

- If you feel intimidated about painting the patterns, I suggest that you start small, in the middle of the "palm," and work your way out. Most mehndi designs are very organic, and easy enough to draw freehand, or you can just leave the design to your imagination.

- Place ½ to 1 teaspoon black or brown gel food coloring in a condiment cup. Add only a drop or two of water. The food coloring should not be heavily diluted; it needs

to be almost full strength to make a clear, precise line.

- Using a fine-tipped artists' brush, begin painting the design in the center of the cookie. Dip the paintbrush as often as needed to produce a clear, smooth line. Retrace dry brushstrokes with strokes from a reloaded paintbrush.

- Some mehndi designs have specific meanings. I used the lotus flower because it represents transformation. The lotus flower has to rise from the muddy depths of the pond before it can reach the surface to bloom.

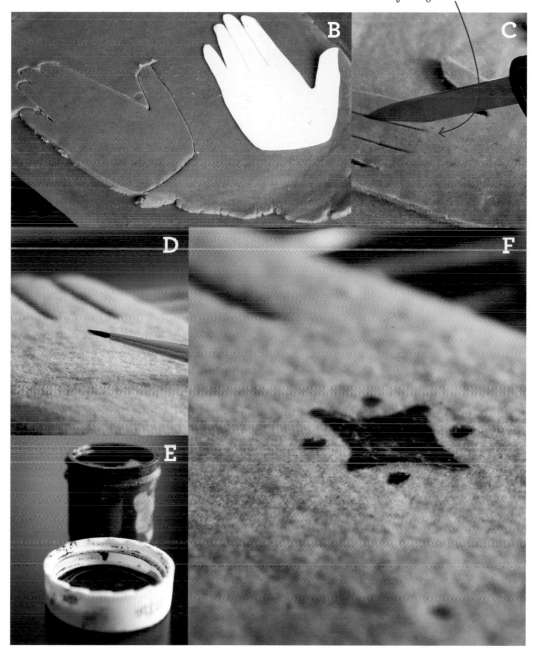

don't cut all the way through—just make a line

A. Chill the dough between wax paper. B. Lay the hand template on top of the chilled dough and cut around it with a sharp knife. C. Make impressions with the back of the knife. D. Use small, soft bristle brushes, as they are ideal for painting cookies. E. The gel food coloring will provide a bold line. F. Paint simple shapes and dots in the palm of the hand cookie.

MARIMEKKO COOKIES

YIELD: 24 cookies

The inspiration for these bold and colorful cookies came from the simple and elegant textiles by iconic Finnish design company Marimekko. Their bright, colorful fabrics grace clothing, handbags, accessories—even furniture! I've taken a design element from their iconic seventies poppy design, Unikko, and made it edible.

MARIMEKKO COOKIES
- ½ pound (2 sticks) butter, softened
- 1 cup plus 2 tablespoons sugar
- 1 egg, lightly beaten
- 1 teaspoon vanilla extract
- 3 cups all-purpose flour, plus more for rolling
- Pinch of salt

TEMPLATE (see page 262)

ICING
- 3 cups royal icing with meringue powder or egg whites (see page 71)
- Red gel food coloring
- Orange gel food coloring
- Black gel food coloring

Make the cookies:

1. In a mixer with a paddle attachment, mix the butter and sugar together until just incorporated. Do not over-mix at this stage, or the cookies may spread while baking.

2. Add the egg and vanilla extract. Mix again on low speed, stopping to scrape down the sides of the bowl intermittently as needed.

3. Add the flour and salt. Mix on low speed until the dough comes together.

4. Turn the dough out onto a sheet of plastic wrap and form into a ball. The dough will not be sticky and should be easy to work with your hands. Wrap tightly and refrigerate for 1 hour.

5. While waiting for the dough to chill, trace the flower template on a piece of wax paper. Cut out the wax-paper flower and use as a template, or make a sturdier template by using the wax paper flower to trace on heavy-grade craft paper.

6. Line two cookie sheets with parchment.

7. When it is thoroughly chilled, place the dough on a well-floured surface and knead slightly, squeezing it with your hands to flatten the ball into a disc. With a floured rolling pin, roll the dough evenly to a ¼-inch thickness.

8. Lay the flower template (see page 262) on the dough. Using a sharp, plain-edge knife, cut around the template and transfer the cookie to the prepared pans.

GRAPHIC DESIGN

Busy florals and extensively elaborate designs are too intricate and time-consuming to replicate in cookie form. Choose a single design element from a textile or wallpaper to replicate instead of the entire pattern.

9. Refrigerate the cutouts for 30 minutes. This will help the cookies maintain a crisp shape during baking.

10. Preheat the oven to 350°F.

11. Bake the cookies for 15 to 20 minutes, or until golden brown around the edges.

12. Let cool on the baking sheet for 5 minutes. Transfer to a wire rack. Decorate cookies when completely cooled.

Prepare the icing:

1. Divide the icing into four batches.

2. Bring one batch of icing to soft-peak consistency by stirring in water, a few drops at a time. Tint this batch red.

3. Bring three batches of icing to flood consistency by stirring in more water, a few drops at a time. Tint one batch red, one orange, and one black.

4. Transfer each batch of icing to a piping bag fitted with a size 4 plain piping tip. Close the end of the bag tightly with a rubber band

and stand each piping bag in a tall glass with a moist paper towel in the bottom to prevent the icing from drying out and the tip from clogging.

Decorate the cookies:

1. Draw the flower's outline with red soft-peak icing. Remember to hold the piping tip above the cookie and let the icing fall into place. Let the outline set for a few minutes to harden.

2. Using the red flood-consistency icing, fill in the soft-peak outline. Pick the cookie up and very gently shake it to settle the flood icing and smooth out any imperfections. Let the icing harden, 4 hours or overnight.

3. When the icing is solid, apply a large dot of black flood icing slightly off center and let harden.

4. When the black icing is dry, pipe orange icing around the black dot.

5. While the orange icing is still wet, drag a toothpick through it, pulling it away from the center to feather the icing outward.

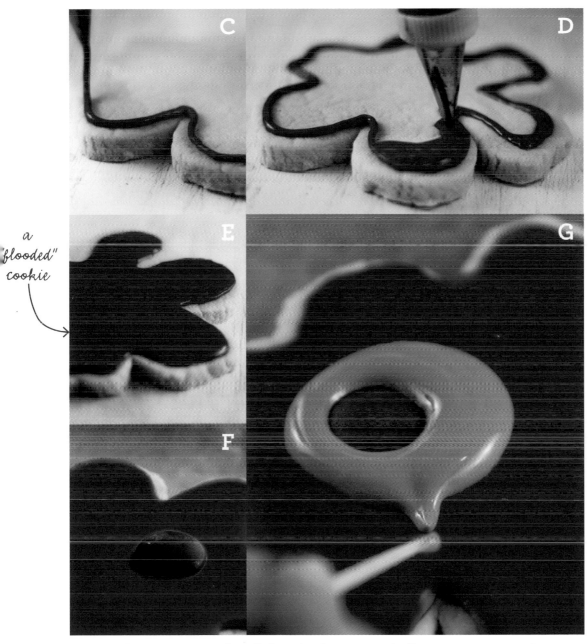

a "flooded" cookie

A. Place a flower template on the rolled out dough. **B.** Cut out the flower. **C.** Create an outline using soft-peak icing. **D.** Fill in the outline with flood icing. **E.** An iced cookie needs plenty of time to dry before you add the embellishments. **F.** Make a black dot at the flower's center. **G.** Pull the orange icing into points with a toothpick.

POSTCARD COOKIES

YIELD: 12 cookies

Stamping is one of the easiest and most satisfying art techniques. Just choose a rubber stamp that suits your aesthetic, and with the addition of ink and paper, you're ready to start creating. I've found a way to employ stamping techniques with simple sugar cookies that transforms them into true works of art. The magic ingredient that makes this possible is *wafer paper.*

Wafer paper is an edible, tasteless potato starch that looks much like a sheet of white copy paper. When applied to icing with a little corn syrup or piping gel, it melds with the icing's surface with barely a trace. Once a professional's secret, it is now accessible to the home baker. Countless online sources sell wafer paper, or you can walk into any bakery that specializes in custom printed cookies and ask them to sell you a few plain sheets.

Begin these cookies a couple of days before you'll need them. The royal icing requires an extended drying time.

POSTCARD COOKIES

- 1 recipe chilled simple sugar cookie dough (see page 14)
- 3 cups white royal icing, flood consistency (see pages 70–71)
- 6 sheets plain wafer paper
- Piping gel or corn syrup
- Nonpareils or other embellishments

EQUIPMENT

- Construction paper or other heavy-weight paper
- High-quality liquid food coloring, such as LorAnn brand
- 2 to 3 small flat-head artist or craft paintbrushes
- Preferably new or clean rubber stamps
- Food-writer pens

Prepare the cookies:

1. Begin this project by cutting two postcard-size (4 x 6 inch) pieces of poster board or construction paper. One piece will be your template for cutting the sugar-cookie dough; reserve the other piece for later use. Line 2 baking sheets with parchment paper. Preheat the oven to 350°F.

2. Roll the cookie dough to a ¼-inch thickness and use one 4 x 6-inch poster-board card as a template to cut out the cookies, flouring your knife after each cutting. Chill cut-outs for 30 minutes in the refrigerator.

3. Bake for 15 to 20 minutes, or until golden brown around the edges

4. While the cookies bake, prepare the royal icing as directed on pages 70–71, half to flood consistency, and half to soft-peak consistency. Transfer to a piping bag fitted with the size 3 tip. When the cookies are baked and cooled, outline the outer edge of each cookie with soft-peak royal icing; let stand 10 minutes for the outlined edge to set. Fill in the interior area of the postcard with flood icing. Very gently hold the cookie by the edges and shake or tap gently to settle the flood icing and smooth out any imperfections.

5. Let the cookies dry completely, 8 hours or overnight.

Stamp the wafer paper:
1. While waiting for the cookies to dry, you can begin stamping the wafer paper. Using the reserved piece of heavy 4 x 6-inch paper as a guide, cut twelve 4 x 6-inch pieces from the 6 sheets of wafer paper. Reserve the scraps for blotting paintbrushes and testing stamps.

2. Place the 4 x 6-inch poster-board template under one of the pieces of wafer paper before you stamp. This will catch any bleed-through ink and save the surface you are working on from being stained.

3. Put a small amount of food coloring in a condiment cup or other small container.

4. Prepare the rubber stamp by dipping a small flat-head paintbrush into the "ink" and press the brush to the side of the dish, releasing most of the food coloring back into the container.

5. Paint food coloring onto the raised areas on the rubber stamp, being careful not to over-saturate. Excessive moisture will melt the wafer paper and render it unusable. I recommend testing the stamp on the scraps of wafer paper until you get a feel for how much ink is necessary to make a good impression. Wafer paper has a shiny side and a textured side. Use the shiny side of the paper to stamp on.

> ### DRY-BRUSH
> A painting technique in which the artist's brush is dry or barely damp, then loaded with color and brushed onto a surface. Luster dust can be dry-brushed on finished cookies to lightly color in stamped pictures.

6. Once you have inked the stamp, hold it on the paper for 2 to 3 seconds. Gently peel the stamp away from the wafer paper. You should have a beautiful, crisp impression.

7. Store the dried stamped wafer papers in a zip-top sandwich bag until ready for use. Wafer paper is perishable, and when not kept in airtight packaging it is prone to dry and may crack during application.

Apply the wafer paper:
1. Before applying the paper to the cookie surface, trim the wafer paper edges to fit just inside the white royal icing area.

2. Working on a piece of parchment paper, apply a thin coat of piping gel or corn syrup over the surface of the icing.

3. Lay the wafer paper on top, pressing gently and smoothing away any air bubbles with your fingers.

4. Flip the cookie over, wafer paper side down. This will help the wafer paper melt into the icing and maintain a flat, even surface. Wait 30 minutes before turning the cookie right side up. Allow the cookie to dry completely, about 4 hours.

soft peak outline

A. Outline the cookies and flood them with royal icing. B. Paint the rubber stamp with food coloring using an artist's brush. C. Apply the stamped wafer paper to the iced cookie with corn syrup.

EMBELLISHMENT IDEAS

- The cookies look best when the edges are finished with a little embellishment. This could be a simple outline of icing in a bold color, or a silver dragée frame, which can be glued on with a little leftover royal icing. Other embellishments may be placed on the surface of the cookie with the same gluing technique.

- Address or message lines can be drawn on with a ruler or other straightedge as a guide. Fun messages can be penned on with food-writer markers.

- Store the cookies in an airtight container for up to 2 weeks.

STRAWBERRY MOUSSE WITH *JOCONDE* CAKE

YIELD: 8 servings

Stencil paste is the same material used to make sculptural *tuile* cookies. Here, it is used to decorate *joconde* cake. (*Joconde* is a sponge cake made with almond flour and baked thin so it can be used to line a charlotte mold.)

I've made two versions that are easy to replicate. The first is striped, and although it may look complex, it's easier than you'd think! You'll just need a small offset spatula or pastry comb. The second version is just as easy. I used a piping bag fitted with a small, plain tip and piped freehand the stars and swirls that appear in the baked cake. If you don't like the design you've drawn, scrape the batter from the parchment paper and start again.

CHOCOLATE STENCIL PASTE
- 4 tablespoons butter, softened
- 1 cup confectioners' sugar
- 3 egg whites, at room temperature
- 1 cup all-purpose flour, sifted
- 1½ tablespoons cocoa powder

JOCONDE SHEET CAKE
- 1 cup almond flour
- ¾ cup confectioners' sugar, sifted
- ¼ cup all-purpose flour
- 3 eggs
- 1 egg yolk
- 3 egg whites (½ cup)

- ¼ cup superfine sugar
- 2 tablespoons butter, melted

STRAWBERRY MOUSSE
- 2 tablespoons unflavored powdered gelatin
- ¼ cup cold water
- 2 cups strawberry puree
- ¾ cup superfine sugar
- 1¼ cups heavy cream

EQUIPMENT
- 8 stainless steel 3-inch pastry rings

Make the chocolate stencil paste:

1. Lightly grease a jelly roll pan and line with parchment paper; lightly grease the parchment.

2. In the bowl of a mixer fitted with the paddle attachment, cream the butter and sugar together until the sugar is dissolved.

3. Add the egg whites and mix again until incorporated.

4. Stir in the flour and cocoa powder and stir until just combined.

5. With a small offset spatula, thinly and evenly spread the stencil paste inside the lined jelly roll pan.

6. Wipe the spatula clean and, using the tip, scrape straight lines into the stencil paste, removing long strips of chocolate to achieve the striped look, and cleaning your spatula with each stripe (a pastry comb can also be used). Leftover stencil paste can be baked into cookies (see page 162 for instructions) or saved for future projects.

7. Place the jelly roll pan in the freezer while you prepare the sheet cake.

Make the *joconde* sheet cake:

1. Preheat the oven to 450°F.

2. Using a stand mixer fitted with the paddle attachment, beat the almond flour, confectioners' sugar, all-purpose flour, whole eggs, and egg yolk until combined, stopping to scrape down the sides of the bowl as necessary.

3. In a separate bowl, whip the egg whites with an electric hand mixer. When the egg whites are foamy, gradually add the superfine sugar until a white, shiny meringue forms.

4. With a large rubber spatula, gently fold the meringue into the almond-flour mixture.

5. Add the melted butter and gently fold again, being careful not to deflate the batter.

6. Remove the jelly roll pan from the freezer and pour the *joconde* cake batter on top.

7. Bake for 5 to 8 minutes, or until the cake springs back when pressed in the center. Remove from the oven and let cool slightly.

8. Invert the cake onto a sheet of parchment and carefully peel away the parchment paper. Trim the edges of the cake with a serrated knife. Set aside.

Make the strawberry mousse:

1. In a small bowl, sprinkle the powdered gelatin over the cold water. Let stand until the gelatin has become spongy. Microwave for 10 seconds or until the gelatin has melted into a clear liquid. If you prefer, you can also set the gelatin mixture over a bowl of hot water and stir until dissolved.

2. Combine the strawberry puree and sugar; mix well.

3. Pour in the liquid gelatin mixture. Let stand at room temperature until the mixture begins to thicken, about 20 minutes.

4. Whip the heavy cream until stiff peaks form.

5. Stir the strawberry puree gently to loosen it. With a rubber spatula, fold 2 to 3 tablespoons of whipped cream into the fruit puree to relax it. Fold in the remaining whipped cream, mixing until just combined and no dark streaks of fruit puree remain. Set aside.

Assemble the cakes:

1. Place the pastry rings on a large flat plate or pan and line them with parchment paper.

2. Cut the striped *joconde* into 1½-inch strips and cut to fit the inside of the pastry rings. Use a small round or other shaped cookie cutter to cut pieces out of the cake scraps for garnish.

3. Fill each ring with about ½ cup mousse, until the mousse is at least ½ inch higher than the top edge of the cake. Refrigerate until set.

4. To serve, put a mouse cake on a serving plate and gently pull the ring off the dessert. Carefully pull the parchment paper off the sides of the cake. Garnish with small cake cutouts and serve immediately.

JOCONDE TIPS

- Cut one strip to size, and then use that piece as a template to cut the others.

- Freeze the cakes for easy unmolding. Let thaw in the refrigerator before serving.

- An alternative to the striped *joconde* is simply drawing shapes and patterns freehand onto parchment paper using a piping bag filled with stencil paste before pouring the cake batter into the jelly roll pan. A size 3 or 5 plain piping tip works best for drawing.

- Templates can be made by tracing designs onto the parchment paper with pencil. Make sure you use the parchment paper side opposite the pencil markings when baking your cake.

A. Scrape away lines of stencil paste in the parchment-lined pan. **B.** The baked and trimmed *joconde* sheet. **C.** Cut strips of *joconde* cake to fit inside the pastry rings. **D.** Line the walls of the pastry ring with the strips. **E.** The ends should meet inside the ring. **F.** Instead of stripes, stencil paste can be piped into swirls. **G.** Fill the cake rings with strawberry mousse. **H.** Top with fanned, sliced strawberries or other fruit.

HEART TEA CAKES

YIELD: 12 teacakes or 16 mini-muffins

These simple yet beautiful tea cakes were made in petit four pans, but they can be baked in any shape mold or tart pan. Teacakes are best served the day they are made.

½ cup almond flour or finely ground
   almonds
¼ pound (1 stick) butter
¼ cup all-purpose flour
¾ cup confectioners' sugar
⅛ teaspoon salt

3 egg whites
Seeds of 1 vanilla bean
¼ cup seedless jelly; a dark color
   such as blackberry or raspberry
   works best

1. Preheat the oven to 350°F.

2. Place the almond flour spread out in an even layer on a parchment-lined baking sheet and toast in the oven for 6 to 8 minutes, or until lightly browned and fragrant. Remove from the oven and let cool.

3. Increase the oven temperature to 400°F. Place 12 mini-tart molds on a baking sheet or line a mini-muffin tin with paper liners.

4. In a small saucepan, melt the butter over medium heat. Line a mesh sieve with cheese cloth or a coffee filter, and place over a small bowl. Once the butter has melted, allow it to come to a boil. Swirl the pan occasionally; do not stir. As the butter boils, you will notice foam on the butter's surface.

5. Continue to cook until the butter becomes clear and the milk solids have dropped to the bottom of the pan; cook until the butter solids turn light golden brown and the butter is nutty and fragrant.

6. Remove from the heat and immediately pour through the mesh sieve into the bowl,

7. Let cool to room temperature. Measure out ⅓ cup of the browned butter and reserve. Use the remaining butter to grease the molds, using a pastry brush.

8. In a large bowl, whisk together the flour, almond flour, confectioners' sugar, and salt.

9. Make a small well in the center of the flour mixture, and fold in the egg whites, seeds from the vanilla bean, and reserved ⅓ cup of browned butter.

10. Fill each mold.

11. In a small bowl, heat the jelly in the microwave at full power in 30-second intervals. Heat the jelly just enough to loosen it, so that it still has some body when stirred and is not completely liquid.

12. Place the melted jelly in a disposable piping bag (a zip-top sandwich bag will work too) and snip off the tip.

13. Pipe 1 dime-size dot of jelly on top of each unbaked teacake.

14. Gently pull the pointed tip of a skewer or toothpick through the batter and down the center of the jelly dot, creating a heart shape in the batter.

A. Fill petit fours pans with the batter. **B.** Pull a skewer through the dots of melted jelly. **C.** An unbaked heart *financier*. **D.** A serving tray full of lovely heart tea cakes.

15. Bake for about 12 minutes, or until the cakes have become light brown on top and are springy to the touch.

16. Remove from the oven and let cool on a wire rack completely before unmolding.

QUEEN OF HEARTS COOKIES

YIELD: Approximately 15 cookies

A dear friend asked me to make treats for her daughter's *Alice in Wonderland*–themed birthday party. I immediately envisioned a cookie with the Queen of Hearts' aristocratic face on it. Perhaps by making the queen's head into cookies, I was exacting a little table-turning revenge on behalf of the queen's court. It can take a while for the icing to dry, so plan ahead.

QUEEN OF HEARTS COOKIES
- ½ pound (2 sticks) butter, softened
- 1 cup plus 2 tablespoons sugar
- 1 egg, lightly beaten, at room temperature
- 1 teaspoon vanilla extract
- 3 cups all-purpose flour, plus more for rolling
- Pinch of salt

ICING
- 4 cups confectioners' sugar, sifted
- 3 tablespoons meringue powder
- ½ cup warm water, plus more for thinning the icing

- ½ teaspoon clear extracts (lemon, orange, almond)
- Black gel food coloring
- Red gel food coloring
- Small white pearl dragées

TEMPLATE (see page 263)

EMBELLISHMENT
- ½ cup ready-made white fondant, rolled to ⅛-inch thick
- Black food writer
- Blue luster dust
- Corn syrup or piping gel
- Heart confetti quins

Make the cookies:

1. Line 2 baking sheets with parchment paper.

2. In a mixer fitted with the paddle attachment, mix the butter and sugar together until just incorporated. Do not over-mix at this stage, or the cookies may spread while baking.

3. Add the beaten egg and vanilla extract. Mix again on low speed, stopping to scrape down the sides of the bowl intermittently as needed.

4. Add the flour and salt; mix on low speed until a firm dough is formed.

5. Turn the dough out onto a sheet of plastic wrap and form into a ball. The dough will not be sticky and should be easy to work with your hands. Wrap tightly and refrigerate for 1 hour.

6. Working on a well-floured surface, knead the dough slightly, squeezing it with your hands to flatten the ball into a disc.

7. With a floured rolling pin, roll the dough evenly to a ¼-inch thickness. For perfectly even

dough, you may use two flat ¼-inch dowels as guides on either side of your workspace or rolling-pin guide bands.

8. With a 4- or 6-inch heart-shaped cookie cutter, cut the dough and transfer the cutouts to the prepared baking sheets. Large cookie cutters are better for this project, as they give lots of room for drawing and detail.

9. Refrigerate the cutouts for 30 minutes. This will help the cookies maintain a crisp shape during baking.

10. Preheat the oven to 350°F.

11. Bake the cookies for 15 to 20 minutes, or until golden brown around the edges.

12. Let cool on the baking sheet for 5 minutes. Transfer to a wire rack to cool completely before decorating.

Note: Shortbread or gingerbread dough may be used in place of the sugar cookie dough.

Make the icing:
1. In the bowl of an electric mixer with the whisk attachment, stir the confectioners' sugar and meringue powder on low speed until combined. (For royal icing made with fresh egg whites, see page 71.)

2. Add the water and beat on medium to high speed until very stiff peaks form, 5 to 7 minutes.

3. Add desired flavoring and beat on low until combined.

4. Divide the icing into thirds. Bring one-third of the icing to soft-peak consistency by stirring in water, a few drops at a time, and the rest of the icing to flood consistency with a bit more water. (See instructions on page 70.)

5. Tint the soft-peak portion black, leave one flood portion white, and tint the remaining flood portion red.

SKETCHING

· Sketching is a quick way to execute an idea for later use. I find this particularly helpful when designing cookies. Trace a cookie-cutter shape onto a plain sheet of paper and sketch design ideas inside the outline.

· Since each element of this cookie is hand-drawn, each face will be a little different.

6. Place the icing in the piping bags fitted with the size 3 piping tips. Tightly close each piping bag with a rubber band and rest each in a tall glass with a damp paper towel in the bottom to prevent the icing from hardening in the tip.

Ice and decorate the cookies:
1. Outline the heart with black icing. Draw the outline of the queen's face in the same color. The face should be drawn slightly off center toward the right side of the cookie. Let the icing dry slightly.

2. Fill in the face outline with white flood icing. Gently tap the cookie on the work surface to smooth the flood icing.

3. Fill in the remaining space with red flood icing; tap the cookie gently to settle the icing. This will be the queen's hair. Use a toothpick to push the icing into the small gaps that need to be filled. Before the icing sets, place a small pearl dragée "earring" to the right of the cookie, where the ear arches outward. Let the icing dry completely. For best results, let dry overnight.

4. Cut out the templates (see page 263) for the queen's eyes and lay them on a small piece of rolled fondant. Using an X-Acto knife or small paring knife, cut 20 pairs of eye shapes from rolled fondant.

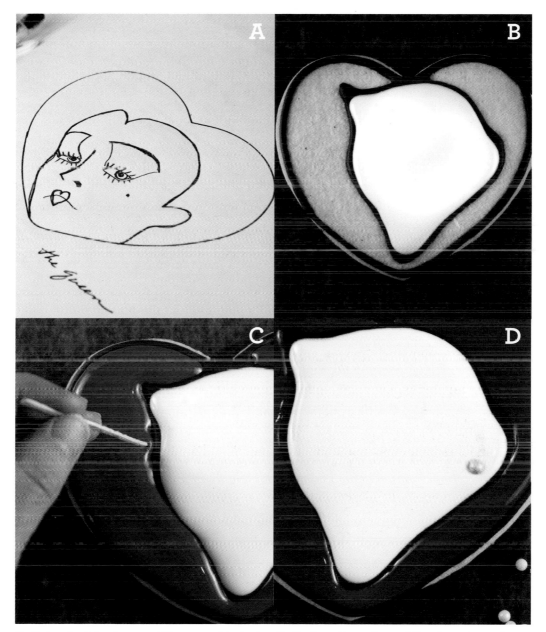

A. A sketch of the Queen of Hearts cookie design. B. Outline the cookie and flood it with royal icing. C. Use a toothpick to push icing into gaps near the outline. D. Place a pearl dragée "earring" into the icing while it is wet.

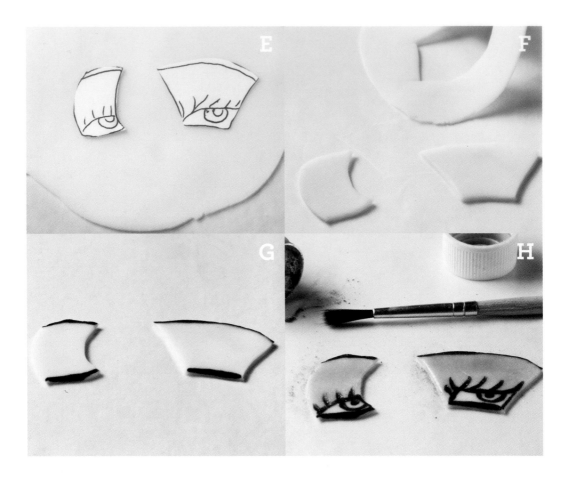

5. Outline the upper and lower edge of the fondant pieces with the black food writer. Draw the outline of the eyes. Add pupils and irises by drawing a half circle with a dot in the center. Add the eyelashes.

6. Apply the luster dust with a small dry artists' brush to the area above the eyes.

7. Lightly brush the back of the fondant pieces with corn syrup or piping gel. Position the pieces on the queen's face.

8. Using the black food writer, draw the queen's nose. Think of it as an upside-down seven (7). Just beside the nose to the right, draw a small dot for her nostril. Below the nose, draw a small frown.

9. Apply a tiny drop of white flood icing to the middle of the frown and place a heart confetti quin over the icing dot.

10. Using the food writer, draw squiggly lines on the red part of the cookie to give the queen's hair texture. For the finishing touch, use the food writer to make a beauty mark (a small dot) under the queen's right eye.

11. Let the cookies stand until the heart sugar confetti and fondant eye pieces have set, approximately 1 hour.

E. Place the eye templates on a small piece of rolled fondant. F. Use an X-Acto knife to cut out the eye pieces. G. Use color writer pens are to outline the top and bottom of the eye pieces. H. Draw the eyes, and brush luster dust onto the "eyelids." I. "Glue" the eye pieces on the face, but only after the icing is dry. J. Use heart confetti quins to create a queenly pout. K. Use a black food writer to embellish her hair.

PLAID SWEATER COOKIES

YIELD: 20 to 24 cookies

Fall brings many beautiful changes into our lives. Colorful leaves and sweater weather are two of my favorites, but number one on my list would have to be autumnal baking. The seasonal spices and ingredients lend a special warmth to homes with apple crumble or pumpkin pie in the oven.

These cute checkered spice cookies are a fun way to celebrate the season with plenty of eye appeal. The pattern may look complex, but the technique is very simple. A cookie cutter 3 inches or larger is preferred, as it gives adequate room to apply the pattern. If you can't find a shirt-shape cookie cutter, leaf-shape cutters or simple shapes such as circles and squares make a pretty plaid cookie.

PLAID SWEATER COOKIES
- 1 recipe spice cookie dough, enough for approximately 20 cookies (see page 100)

FONDANT
- ¾ pound ready-made white fondant icing
- Confectioners' sugar as needed
- ¼ teaspoon moss green gel food coloring

RED AND WHITE ROYAL ICING
- 4 cups confectioners' sugar, sifted
- 3 tablespoons meringue powder
- ½ cup warm water, plus more as needed
- ½ teaspoon clear extract (lemon, orange, almond)
- ½ to 1 teaspoon Christmas red gel food coloring

EQUIPMENT
- Shirt-shape cookie cutter
- Small flat-head paintbrush
- Corn syrup or piping gel
- Small X-Acto knife
- Tweezers and large white nonpareils (optional)

Make the cookies:

1. Follow the recipe and baking instructions for the mehndi hand cookies (see page 100), but cut out sweater-shaped cookies with a 3-inch cutter.

Prepare the fondant:

1. Knead the fondant slightly to make it pliable. If it is sticky, dust your work surface with a little confectioners' sugar and knead a little of the sugar into the fondant.

2. When the fondant is soft and no longer sticky, place the gel coloring in the center of the fondant. Knead the food coloring into the fondant until the color is uniform and no white streaks remain. Place the fondant in a zip-top bag with the air removed and set aside.

Note: Wear disposable plastic gloves to protect your hands from being stained.

Make the royal icing:

1. In the bowl of an electric mixer fitted with the whisk attachment, stir the confectioners' sugar and meringue powder on low speed until combined. (For royal icing made with fresh egg whites, see page 71.)

2. Add the water and beat on medium to high speed until very stiff peaks form, 5 to 7 minutes.

3. Add the flavoring and beat on low until combined.

4. Bring the icing to soft-peak consistency by stirring in more water, a few drops at a time.

5. Divide the icing in half, and tint one portion with red gel food coloring; the other half remains white.

6. Place the icing in two piping bags fitted with size 3 piping tips. Tightly close each piping bag with a rubber band and rest the bags in tall glasses with a damp paper towel in the bottom to prevent the icing from hardening in the tip.

Note: Royal icing hardens very quickly, so it should not be left in the mixing bowl uncovered. Drape a damp tea towel over the mixing bowl to prevent icing from drying out.

Assemble the cookies:

1. On a clean, smooth surface, roll the fondant to a ⅛-inch thickness. Cut the fondant with the same cookie cutters used to cut the spice-cookie dough.

2. Set the cutouts aside and reroll the fondant. Continue cutting until you have 20 to 24 pieces.

3. Sparingly brush the backs of the cutouts with a little piping gel or corn syrup. Apply the brushed cutouts to the cookies, gently pressing

the fondant and lining up the edges as evenly as possible.

4. To pipe the plaid, begin by piping three vertical white stripes on the fondant surface.

5. Pipe three red horizontal stripes very closely together in the upper half of the cookie, saving a bit of space at the neckline.

6. Pipe three more red horizontal stripes very closely together on the lower portion of the cookie.

7. Pipe 2 vertical lines (3 if you have room) down the center between the three white lines and intersecting the red horizontal lines. Repeat this step on the other side of the cookie.

8. Pipe white lines horizontally across the middle and bottom of the cookie, intersecting the 3 vertical red lines and the 3 vertical white lines.

9. Pipe white icing dots, or place tiny white nonpareils at the intersection of each red line and at the shirt cuffs.

10. Fashion a little collar from leftover fondant. The neck portion of the cookie cutter can be used to cut the fondant so it fits perfectly onto the cookie. Use an X-Acto knife to cut the shape of the collar. A nonpareil makes a cute button in the center of the collar. Use a pair of tweezers to press the candy into the fondant, or pipe a dot of white royal icing instead.

Once you have the basic tartan well practiced, have fun experimenting with your own ideas in different hues and patterns.

just a little here and there

A. Knead green food coloring into the fondant. **B.** Use the same cookie cutter to cut the dough and the fondant. **C.** Apply corn syrup to the back of the fondant cut-out. **D.** Pipe straight lines across the cookie. **E.** Pipe lines close together to create a tartan effect. **F.** Use nonpareils or piped dots of icing as buttons.

VIKING WEDDING CAKE

YIELD: Approximately 50 2-to-3-inch-piece servings

This cake is known by many names: *kransekake*, Norwegian crown cake, and Viking wedding cake. It is traditional Scandinavian wedding fare that is 18 tiers tall and is much more like a cookie in texture than a cake.

These impressive tiers are usually decorated with colorful Scandinavian flags, but I chose two simple Viking banners to adorn this wedding cake. The first is the raven flag, which was usually flown during a long voyage. The second is a Viking compass. It is a rune said to have magical powers to help those in rough weather find their way. I believe both symbols are appropriate for those embarking on the journey of matrimony.

Note: *Kransekake* ring molds are concentric-circle molds available online and at some specialty cooking stores. If you can't find the rings, simply mark off 18 circles on parchment paper, beginning with a 10–inch circle, and decrease the size by ¼ inch each subsequent circle down to 2 inches in diameter. Employing several baking sheets will make this task easier.

CAKE RINGS
1 pound almond flour, or 1 pound blanched whole almonds ground fine in a food processor
1 pound confectioners' sugar
4 egg whites

GLAZE
2 cups confectioners' sugar
1 egg white
½ teaspoon lemon juice

TEMPLATE (see page 265)

VIKING BANNERS
½ cup ready-made gum paste (pastillage)
Black food writer pen
2 tablespoons candy melts or almond bark
2 large wooden skewers or lollipop sticks

EQUIPMENT
Kransekake ring molds

Make the cake rings:

1. Preheat the oven to 300°F. Grease the *kransekake* molds or prepare the parchment sheets as described above.

2. Fill a saucepan one-third full of water and set over medium heat. Bring to a simmer.

3. In a large heatproof bowl, toss together the almond flour and confectioners' sugar.

4. Stir the egg whites into the almond flour mixture and continue to stir until a thick batter is formed.

5. Place the bowl of batter over the simmering pot of liquid, stirring constantly and heating until batter is warm and loses its stiffness, approximately 5 minutes if you're using a glass or ceramic bowl and less for stainless steel.

the Viking Cake ring molds

A. Mix the confectioners' sugar and almond flour. **B.** Mix the dry ingredients with a whisk or by hand. **C.** Mixed dough should look like this. **D.** Grease the ring molds so they are ready to be filled. **E.** Pipe the batter into the forms. **F.** Apply icing to glue the rings of this many-tiered cake together. **G.** Stack the rings from largest to smallest.

This will make it possible to pipe through a piping bag.

6. Transfer the batter to a large piping bag.

7. Pipe the batter into the greased *kransekake* rings or onto the marked parchment.

8. Bake for 30 to 35 minutes.

9. Let the cake rings cool in the *kransekake* molds or on the baking sheets until completely cool before glazing.

10. To make the glaze, whisk together the confectioners' sugar, egg white, and lemon juice until a thin white glaze forms.

11. Transfer to a piping bag fitted with a size 3 tip and apply the icing in a zigzag pattern across the largest cake tier.

12. Stack the next smallest cake tier on top, allowing the glaze to anchor the tier in place. Repeat the glazing and stacking process with the remaining tiers. Let cake stand uncovered at room temperature while banners are being made.

Make the Viking banners:

1. Roll the gum paste out to a ¼-inch thickness.

2. Cut 1 piece of gum paste into a 2 x 3-inch rectangle. Cut 1 piece of gum paste into a 3 x 3-inch square. Let the gum paste dry until completely hardened, 4 hours or overnight.

3. Using a black food marker, draw the raven banner according to the template (see page 265) on the 2 x 3-inch piece of gum paste. Draw the Viking compass on the 3 x 3-inch piece of gum paste according to the template. When the ink is dry, turn both banners facedown.

4. Melt the candy melts at 30-second intervals in the microwave at full power until smooth.

5. Dip one end of each skewer into the melted candy and lay one on the backs of each banner.

6. When the banners are dry, place the skewers in the opening formed by the cake rings at the top of the structure.

SCULPTURE

Sculpture is the process of creating three-dimensional works of art. This can be achieved through carving, modeling, constructing, and casting. In this chapter, we'll use all of these techniques to give desserts shape and dimension.

A serrated knife is used to carve a square cake into the shape of a book before it is covered with fondant.

CARVING

Carving is a subtractive form of sculpting, as the artist removes or eliminates parts of the material being carved. Like any other form of carving, cake carving is an intuitive process. You must see the desired form within the cake before putting a knife to it. Templates are of little help when creating three-dimensional sculptures; instead, you must imagine the shape before you carve it.

Follow these steps when planning a carving project:

1. Make a cake with a dense crumb. *Madeira* cake and batters for tiered cakes are both good choices.

2. Plan ahead. Make the cake a day ahead of time. This gives you ample time to plan the design and carve the cake to perfection.

3. After the cake is removed from the oven, let it cool, and then place it in an airtight container for several hours. This will allow the cake's dense crumb to develop fully.

4. Choose a cake board or serving platter before beginning the carving process.

5. If you plan to carve multiple pieces for stacking or piecing together, start with the largest piece first. This will help you carve the other pieces to the appropriate size in relation to the largest piece.

6. Use serrated knives. Use large knives to carve the cake into separate pieces and to carve out large pieces. Use small knives for detail work and fine-tuning.

7. When carving, remove portions of cake a little at a time until you achieve the desired

shape. It is difficult to correct overcarving, so this is a very important rule to follow.

8. If designing a large vertical cake, insert wooden dowels into the cake for extra support.

9. Cut the shape, in general, a little smaller than you imagine the finished product will be. Buttercream or fondant or both will be added to the equation and will add mass to the cake.

10. Carved cakes are usually frosted with buttercream and then covered with rolled fondant. Use your fingers to press the fondant into the details carved into the cake. Do this with a gentle touch. Even though fondant is very malleable, it is easy to accidentally poke a finger through the surface.

HAND-MODELING

Modeling is the building of forms by hand. Instead of clay, our media are fondant, gum paste, and edible modeling clays. Unlike carving, modeling is an additive process, and corrections can be easily made. (In contrast, carved media cannot be put back together, at least not easily.)

There are different elements to hand modeling that will help you achieve the sculpture you desire. Before you begin, have plenty of your sculpting media ready. Work on a clean, flat surface. A cutting board is ideal to avoid staining and damage to countertops and tables.

Note: When hand-modeling three-dimensional objects, place a mirror behind the object so you can see it on all sides. It's easy to spend lots of time perfecting one side, only to turn the object around to find that the other side has become misshapen.

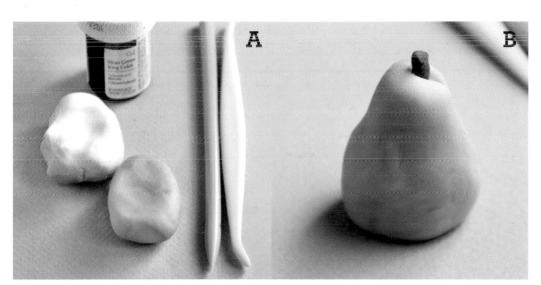

A. Food coloring, fondant, and fondant sculpting tools can be used to create a lifelike, hand-modeled pear. **B.** Making this pear is simple—just use your hands to mold it into shape.

ARMATURE

An armature is the inner skeleton of a molded sculpture. It is usually a wire form that artists use for support when sculpting a piece with appendages. Armatures are only occasionally used in confections that the home baker creates. Wooden dowels, toothpicks, licorice, hard candies, and even marshmallows can form an inner skeleton on which to sculpt.

BUILDING

Building is the process of adding more fondant, gum paste, or clay to the form you are modeling. Layering or adding small pieces onto the form can help you achieve the shape you desire. Also, pieces can be sculpted individually and then assembled, or "built." For example, if you are making a character for a child's cake, you don't have to sculpt the entire form from one piece of fondant. Many pieces,—the head, torso, arms, and legs—can be sculpted individually and pressed together to form the whole.

MANIPULATING

Manipulating is the process of pushing, pinching, pulling, impressing, smoothing, and texturing—anything you do to move the media (fondant, for example) around in an attempt to achieve a certain shape. This can be done with your fingers, hands, and sculpting tools. Fondant-sculpting tools can be purchased for manipulating pastes and clays, but simple household objects such as toothpicks and cutlery can also be used in the same manner.

SUBTRACTING

Carving can also be done when hand-modeling. Unlike cake carving, carving in hand-modeling allows you to add pieces if a carving mistake happens. Chocolate modeling clay can be carved away from a form to refine the shape of your work. Fondants and gum pastes can also be subtracted in this way, but they are gummy and often do not cut as cleanly as chocolate modeling clay.

CONSTRUCTING AND ASSEMBLING

A constructed, assembled sculpture is made by putting together various pieces of media. It's almost like making a collage, except in three dimensions. Usually this type of sculpture needs a base, or armature (a skeleton or form),

Meringues are assembled around a devil's food cupcake for a sculptural assembly.

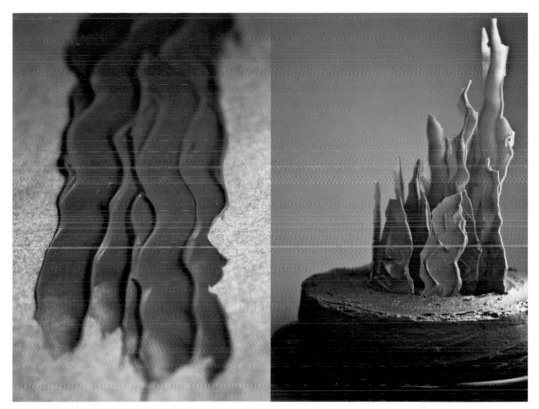

Candy melts are painted on parchment paper in impasto style and then used as a sculptural garnish for a cake.

to build around. In the confectionery world, this could be a cake on which are piled pieces of sculptural meringue or pulled sugar—or a gingerbread house decorated with an assortment of confections.

IMPASTO

Impasto is a form of painting that crosses over into sculpture.

Impasto refers to a technique in which a heavy-bodied paint is laid on a surface very thickly. A palette knife is used to create three-dimensional strokes. When the paint is dry, it is so heavily textured that it appears to be coming out of the surface onto which it has been applied.

In dessert making, the impasto technique can be used with meringue, candy melts, chocolate, and almond bark. These materials can be applied directly to the surface of the blank-canvas dessert (cookies, cakes), or they can be spread on parchment and left to harden. Once hardened, the candy can be lifted from the paper and used as a sculptural garnish for cakes and tarts.

CASTING

Molds are used in casting sculptural confections. If you've ever made molded chocolates or lollipops, then you already have experience with casting.

NEGATIVE MOLDS

The most common type of mold is a negative mold. With this type of casting, you can pour or press material into the cavity, filling the negative space. If you think about it, the confectionery world is full of this type of mold; cake pans, cupcake tins, pudding molds, and madeleine pans are all examples of negative molds. Many materials can be used for this type of casting: chocolate, almond bark, gelatin, custards, and hard candy are just a few.

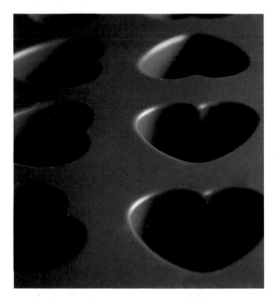

Candy and chocolate molds are negative molds.

SAND CASTING

Anyone can go to a store and buy a candy mold, but here's a fun way to create your own custom negative mold. Sand casting is a method in which an object is pressed into sand and tightly packed to create an impression. For culinary confections, brown sugar is used instead of sand to hold an impression of whatever object you choose. The best impressions are made from objects that have lots of three-dimensional details, like the ridges on the scallop shell used in the example that follows (Chocolate Shells).

Chocolate Shells

- A bowl that is large enough to accommodate the shell (or whatever object you wish to use)
- Enough brown sugar to fill the bowl three-quarters full
- Enough semisweet chocolate chips to fill the impression when melted

1. Fill the bowl three-quarters full of brown sugar and pack lightly.

2. Embed the object in the brown sugar. Press down firmly and pack the brown sugar around the object.

3. Remove the object and view the impression. If it isn't perfect, then fluff the brown sugar and make another impression.

4. Melt the chocolate chips at 30-second intervals in the microwave, stirring between intervals. When smooth, pour the chocolate into the impression.

A. To sand cast a scallop shell, press it into the brown sugar. **B.** It will leave behind a shell-shaped depression. **C.** Fill the depression with melted chocolate. **D.** A beautiful chocolate shell!

5. Freeze until the chocolate has completely hardened.

6. When the chocolate has hardened, remove the cast figure from the bowl of brown sugar and quickly rinse away the excess sugar under a thin stream of cold water. Gently pat the shape dry with a towel or air-dry and use as an embellishment for your choice of confection.

POSITIVE MOLDS

Turn a negative mold upside down, and you will see the positives. Material can be painted on or shaped around a positive mold. For example, *tuile* cookies can be shaped over a cup turned upside down to replicate its shape, creating a *tuile* container.

In the exercise that follows (Chocolate Bowls), inflated balloons are used as positive molds. They are dipped in chocolate, and when the chocolate is set, the balloons are deflated to reveal a perfect chocolate vessel that can hold pudding, berries, whipped cream—whatever your imagination dreams up.

Chocolate Bowls

- 8 to 10 small balloons
- 12 ounces semisweet chocolate chips, melted and cooled slightly
- Parchment paper
- Scissors

1. Inflate the balloons and leave them on a dust-free surface. Balloons have static, so they easily attract particles. Place them on parchment paper or on a very clean platter.

2. Lay several sheets of parchment paper on a flat work surface.

3. Dip a balloon in cooled chocolate. It is important that the chocolate is not too hot; otherwise, the balloons will pop when dipped. Place the dipped balloon on parchment paper.

4. Let the chocolate set at room temperature. When it has hardened, gently use scissors to snip a small hole near the balloon tie-off. Allow the air to escape slowly so it pulls away gently from the chocolate. If the balloon sticks to the chocolate, gently pull it from the sides of the chocolate container with your fingers. Do not pop the balloon with a pin—if it deflates too quickly, the bowl can crack.

Now you are ready to fill your chocolate container and enjoy!

A., B., and C. Once the chocolate-dipped balloon has hardened, slowly release the air from the balloon. Make a small cut near the knot, where the balloon skin isn't so taut. **D.** Beautiful chocolate bowls, made with the positive mold technique!

BANANA PUDDING CAKE

YIELD: 10 servings (refrigerate any unused portions)

This three-layer cake has an outer layer of soft meringue that can be sculpted into swirls, peaks, or vertical stripes. Texturing the meringue is good practice for using a palette knife (in baking, an offset spatula). I encourage you to experiment and take note of the shapes your palette knife makes as you sculpt.

Another fabulous element of this dessert is the custard frosting that lies just beneath the meringue layer. It keeps the cake moist and imparts an authentic banana pudding flavor.

Three seven-inch springform pans were used to create a tall silhouette for this cake. Two 9-inch cake pans could be used if you don't have a smaller size in your collection.

CAKES
- ¼ pound (1 stick) butter, softened
- 1¾ cups sugar
- 3 eggs, at room temperature
- 2 teaspoons vanilla extract
- 2¼ cups all-purpose flour
- 3½ teaspoons baking powder
- 1 teaspoon salt
- 1¼ cups whole milk, at room temperature

CUSTARD FROSTING
- ¾ cup sugar
- 2 heaping tablespoons all-purpose flour
- 1 whole egg
- 1 egg yolk
- 1 cup whole milk
- 2 teaspoons vanilla nut extract
- ¼ pound (1 stick) butter, softened
- 2 tablespoons confectioners' sugar

ASSEMBLY
- 3 small, ripe bananas
- 1 tablespoon lemon juice
- ½ cup graham cracker crumbs (optional)

MERINGUE
- 1 cup egg whites (from 5 or 6 eggs)
- 1 pinch cream of tartar
- 1 cup superfine sugar

Make the three cakes:

1. Preheat the oven to 350°F. Grease the bottom and sides of three 7-inch springform pans (if you don't have 3, you can reuse the ones you have). Line the bottom and sides with parchment paper, and then grease the paper.

2. In the bowl of a standing mixer fitted with the paddle attachment, cream the butter and sugar together.

3. Add the eggs and vanilla and beat until combined.

4. Combine the flour, baking powder, and salt and add to the mixer bowl in three batches, alternating with the milk and beginning and ending with the flour mixture. Scrape down the bowl and beat on high speed for 3 minutes.

5. Divide the batter evenly into pans, or if reusing a pan, fill each pan two-thirds full.

A. Create three layers of butter cake. B. Spread the custard frosting on a layer. C. Stack bananas on top of the custard frosting. D. Stack the cakes with the custard and banana between the layers. E. Tall cakes require extra support, provided here by a plastic straw. F. Cover the entire cake in custard frosting.

6. Bake for 25 to 30 minutes, or until a toothpick comes out clean when inserted into the middle of the cakes.

7. Let the cakes cool slightly in the pans. Remove and let them cool completely on a wire rack.

Make the custard frosting:

1. In a medium saucepan, mix the sugar and flour together.

2. Beat in the whole egg and egg yolk. Add the milk. Mix well.

3. Whisk in the vanilla-nut extract.

4. Place over medium-high heat and whisk while cooking until the mixture begins to boil and thickens just like pudding.

5. Let cool completely.

6. In the bowl of a stand mixer fitted with the whisk attachment, beat the butter and confectioners' sugar together until well combined.

7. Add the cooled custard mixture to the butter mixture. Beat on high speed for 5 to 7 minutes, until thick and spreadable. Set aside.

plastic
straw
to keep
layers
in place

Assemble the cake:

1. Thinly slice the bananas and place in a medium bowl.

2. Toss the bananas with the lemon juice until coated (this prevents the fruit from browning).

3. Line the edges of a serving plate or cake stand with wax paper strips to catch drips and keep the serving plate clean.

4. Place one of the cake layers on the paper and top with a thin layer of custard.

5. Top the custard with half the banana slices.

6. Top the bananas with more custard and set the second cake layer on top.

7. Top the cake with another layer of custard. Add a layer of bananas and top it with more custard. Place the final cake layer on top of the custard.

Note: When making the 7-inch cake, reinforce the middle with a plastic straw. The silhouette is tall and thin, so it requires extra stability. As you push the straw into the middle of the cake, the bananas and custard will want to squeeze out the sides a little. Once the straw is in, gently tuck in any banana slices that are trying to escape. If the straw sticks out of the top, snip it off with a pair of scissors.

8. Coat the entire cake with the custard frosting using an offset spatula. Don't worry about making the icing perfect; this layer will be covered by a thick layer of meringue.

9. Set the cake aside or chill briefly while you make the meringue.

TEXTURE

In art, the word *texture* is used to describe an artwork's visual feel. It is also often used to describe how a three-dimensional surface feels when touched.

Make the meringue and finish and embellish the cake:

1. In a large bowl, whip the egg whites until foamy with an electric hand mixer.

2. Add the cream of tartar and beat on medium speed until soft peaks form.

3. Increase the speed to high and gradually beat in the sugar until the whites are glossy and hold stiff peaks.

4. Coat the entire cake with meringue. Use a small offset spatula as a palette knife to texture the meringue. The technique used on this cake is "pulled meringue." A spatula is pressed flat into the meringue and pulled back to create peaks. Apply texture to the entire cake as desired.

5. If desired, coat the bottom half of the cake with graham cracker crumbs.

6. Remove the wax paper strips from the plate. Brown the textured meringue with a kitchen torch, or if you don't have one you can place the cake under the broiler in the oven. Watch the meringue carefully, as it will brown quickly under such high heat.

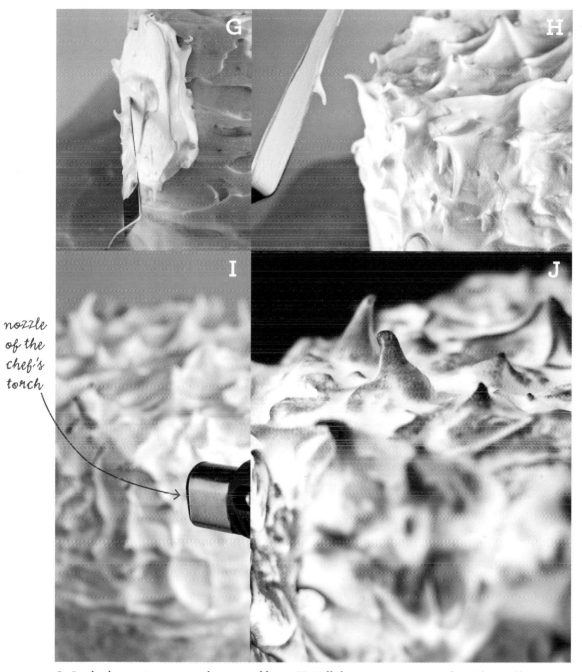

nozzle of the chef's torch

G. Apply the meringue over the custard layer. H. Pull the meringue into peaks with an off-set spatula. I. Use a chef's torch to brown the meringue. J. Caramelized meringue—yum!

DALE CHIHULY-INSPIRED CANDY NESTING BOWLS

YIELD: Enough for up to 12 portions

If you are familiar with the work of Dale Chihuly, then you know of his grand-scale blown-glass installations, squiggly-armed forms, and nesting pieces. Whenever I attend his exhibitions, I am always in awe of his inspired glass masterpieces.

The candy centerpiece I've created is reminiscent of the Chihuly style. Three candy bowls in primary colors (red, blue, yellow) nest to create a rainbow of color. It is especially pretty when sunlit or sitting close to a light source. Crafting the bowls requires no special sculpting talent, but the finished piece looks like a true work of art. Dinner guests may mistake it as such and gasp when you break it into pieces for consumption.

CANDY
- 2 cups sugar
- ⅔ cup water
- ⅔ cup light corn syrup
- 1 teaspoon butter rum candy-flavoring oil
- 10 to 15 drops each red, blue, and yellow liquid food coloring

EQUIPMENT
- Unbleached parchment paper
- Three graduated bowls; I used a 4-inch-wide (across the top) condiment cup, a 5½-inch-wide bowl, and a 7-inch-wide bowl
- Candy thermometer
- 2 heatproof glass measuring cups with pour spout

1. Have ready 3 lengths of parchment, about 12 inches long, set on a flat heatproof surface.

2. Stir the sugar, water, and corn syrup together in a medium-size nonstick saucepan.

3. Place the saucepan over medium-high heat, clip a candy thermometer to the side of the pan, and bring the sugar mixture to a boil.

4. Simmer until the temperature reaches 302°F; this is known as the hard-crack stage.

5. When the required temperature has been reached, remove from the heat.

6. Stir in the candy-flavoring oil.

7. Working quickly, pour ¼ to ⅓ cup hot candy in one of the liquid measures, and stir in the yellow food coloring. The mixture will bubble and begin to thicken.

8. Pour the yellow candy onto one of the parchment sheets. Don't worry if it spreads out and develops "arms," this just adds to the beauty.

9. In the second measuring cup, pour in slightly more candy than you did in the first measuring cup. Add the blue food coloring and mix well. Pour onto a piece of parchment.

10. Add the red food coloring to the remaining candy left in the saucepan, stir well, and pour out onto the third piece of parchment.

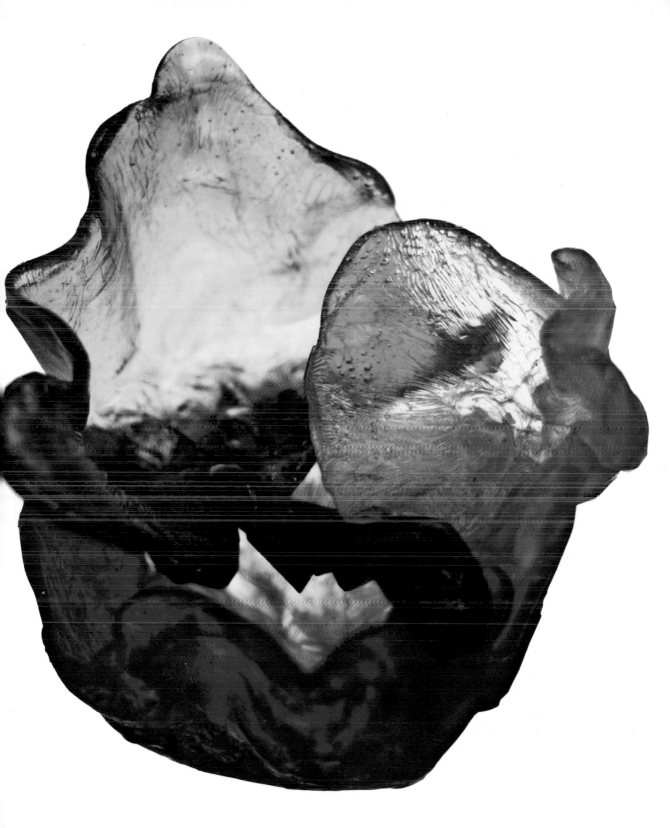

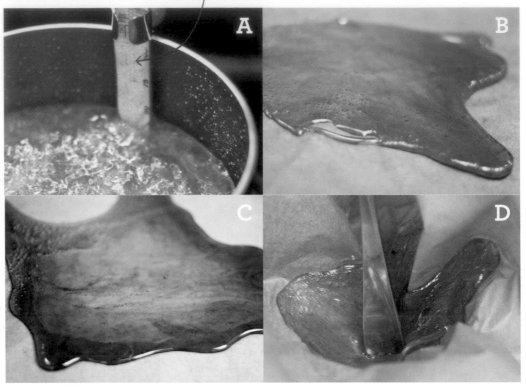

a candy thermometer

A. Boil the sugar mixture. **B. and C.** Pour the yellow and blue candy onto parchment. **D.** When the candy is slightly cooled but still malleable, press it into a bowl using the end of a spoon.

11. Allow the candy to set for 5 to 7 minutes. Gauge the behavior of the candy by lifting one edge of the parchment. The candy is ready to shape when its surface wrinkles on top and the candy does not run when lifted. It will have the consistency of putty and should still be a little hot to the touch. If there is excess parchment around the edges of the candy, carefully trim, leaving enough edge to handle the candy.

12. Pick up the yellow candy parchment by the edges and center it over the smallest bowl's surface. With the handle of a spoon or fork, press the malleable candy down into the bowl, allowing it to wrinkle and ruffle as it naturally wants to.

13. Repeat this process with all the candy, pressing the blue into the medium bowl and the red into the largest bowl, making sure the red piece (or base) has a flat bottom so it will stand on its own. You can flatten the candy by gently pressing it into the bottom of the bowl with a small glass or heatproof cup.

14. Allow the pieces to harden for about 20 minutes.

15. Carefully peel the parchment from the hardened candy.

16. Place the red sculpture on a decorative plate and arrange the graduated bowls, nesting one inside the other.

17. To consume, place one sculpture between two tea towels and break apart with a sturdy metal spatula or a small hammer.

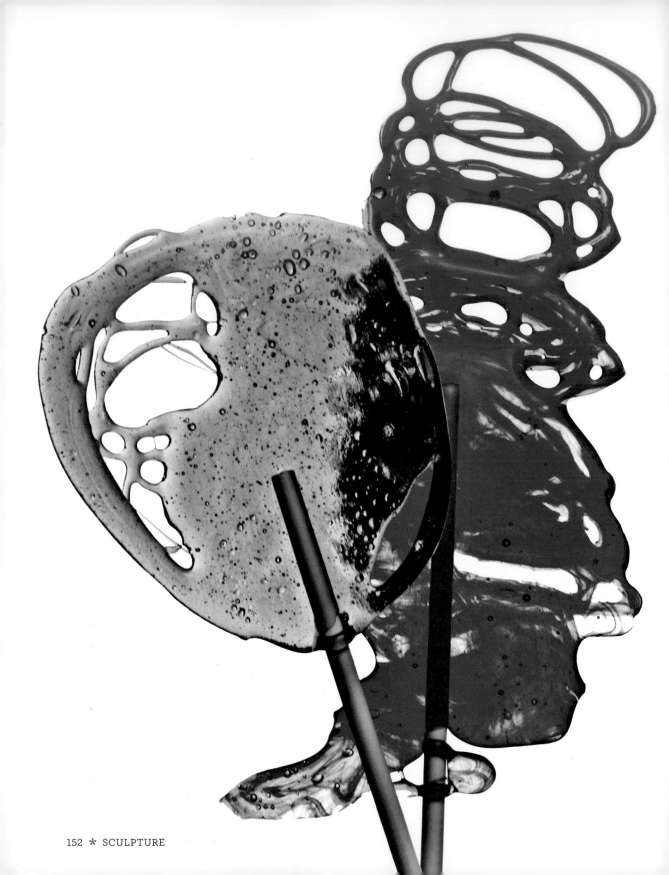

FREE-FORM LOLLIPOPS

YIELD: 15 to 20 lollipops

Free-form art is about being in the moment. It's about letting your creative expression happen naturally and organically. This recipe is a fun exercise in free-form sculpture. As you drizzle the liquid candy over the lollipop sticks, let the colors and shapes develop as they will.

LOLLIPOPS

2 cups sugar
⅔ cup corn syrup
⅔ cup water
½ to 1 dram bottle (⅛ to ¾ teaspoon) clear flavoring oil
Liquid food coloring in blue, red, and yellow

EQUIPMENT

10 lollipop sticks
Unbleached parchment paper
Candy thermometer
2 heatproof glass measuring cups with pour spout
Long wooden skewer

1. Grease 2 large baking sheets with vegetable shortening and line with parchment. Grease the parchment paper. Lay 10 lollipop sticks, staggered, on each piece of parchment.

2. Stir together the sugar, corn syrup, and water in a small saucepan.

3. Clip a candy thermometer to the side of the pan and bring the mixture to a boil over high heat. Continue to heat without stirring until the bubbling mixture reaches the hard-crack stage (302°F).

4. Stir in the flavoring oil. Be extra careful because the mixture will bubble and sputter with this addition.

5. Divide the liquid candy between two heat-safe glass measuring cups.

6. Add a few drops of food coloring to each measure in any combination of the three colors.

7. Swirl the wooden skewer in both mixtures only once or twice. Do not try to achieve a solid color. The idea is to marble the colors.

8. With a metal spoon, scoop candy out of the measure and over one end of the lollipop sticks. Allow the candy to drizzle off the end of the spoon. Move the spoon around, letting the candy fall randomly. Allow the candy to run if it so chooses; it's fun to see what shapes naturally occur.

9. Allow candy to harden, then wrap lollipops in wax paper or cellophane bags and store in an airtight container.

NEGATIVE SPACE

Negative space is a dynamic property in sculpture. Positive spaces are those occupied by the main subjects of the work—in this application, the hard candy. The negative spaces are the areas around and behind the positive spaces—the holes in the hard candy. While making these sculptural lollies, try to create interesting negative space as you drizzle the hot candy into shapes.

SUGARPLUMS

YIELD: 12 sugarplums

"While visions of sugarplums danc'd in their heads..."

   Clement C. Moore's beloved poem "The Night before Christmas" mentions children contentedly dreaming of these delicacies on Christmas Eve. Although quite lovely in taste, I find the classic version of this holiday treat somewhat lacking aesthetically. With a layer of marzipan and sparkling sugar, however, these little hand-sculpted plums are a treat for the eyes as well as the tongue.

SUGARPLUM FILLING
- 8 to 10 dried figs, stems removed
- ⅓ cup slivered almonds
- 3 tablespoons unsweetened cocoa powder
- ¼ cup honey
- ¼ teaspoon almond extract
- Seeds of 1 vanilla bean, or ¼ teaspoon vanilla extract

MARZIPAN COATING
- 8 ounces quality marzipan such as Niederegger Weissbrot, or home-made (see page 78)
- Violet gel food coloring

- Confectioners' sugar, for rolling
- ¼ cup superfine sugar
- ¼ cup large-crystal decorative sugar, plus more for display

PLUM LEAVES
- Green food coloring
- ¼ cup white fondant (see page 74)
- Gold luster dust (optional)
- Chocolate jimmies (for stems)

EQUIPMENT
- Fondant roller
- Small leaf-shaped fondant cutter (optional)
- Soft-hair (sable) paintbrush

Make the sugarplums:

1. In the bowl of a food processor, combine the figs, almonds, and cocoa. Pulse a few times until well minced.

2. Add the honey, almond extract, and vanilla bean seeds and pulse until well combined.

3. Roll into 1-inch balls. Set aside.

Prepare the marzipan and assemble the sugarplums:

1. Color the marzipan with a small amount of violet gel food coloring. Knead until you get a consistent color throughout, with no streaks remaining.

2. Place the marzipan on a clean, flat surface and roll to a ¼-inch thickness with a fondant roller or smooth rolling pin. You may use a light dusting of confectioners' sugar to prevent the marzipan from sticking.

3. Cut small pieces of marzipan and fold them around the sugarplum centers. Pinch off any excess.

4. Form each confection into a plum shape. The top should be slightly pointed to accommodate the stem and leaf. The bottom should be flat enough for the sugarplum to stand upright. Make an indentation vertically down the center of each sugarplum with the back of a knife.

A. Finely grind the filling in a food processor. **B.** Roll the filling into 1-inch balls. **C.** Apply a little food coloring to the marzipan. **D.** Purple marzipan! **E.** Wrap the filling ball in a square of purple marzipan. **F.** Use the back of a knife to make an indention in the marzipan that mimics a plum shape.

5. The marzipan will be naturally oily from the almonds used in the paste. This helps the double coating of sugar adhere to the surface of the sugarplums. First, dip the sugarplums in the superfine sugar; then dip them in the large crystal sugar. This gives them just the right amount of sparkle.

Make the leaves:

1. Mix a small amount of green gel food coloring into the fondant. Roll flat to a ¼-inch thickness with a fondant roller.

2. Using the fondant leaf cutter (or you could cut freehand or use a handmade template)

cut as many leaves as you have sugarplums (10 to 12).

3. Make indentations on the cutouts to represent leaf veins.

4. Dip a small paintbrush in water; then dip it in the luster dust. Coat each leaf lightly for a gilded appearance. Place the fondant leaf atop the sugarplum and anchor it with a chocolate jimmy. The jimmy will press into the soft fondant and marzipan easily.

5. Serve on a platter lined with coarse sugar crystals to resemble snow.

ster dust
dds icy
himmer

G. Coat the sugarplum in sugar. H. Apply a little food coloring to the fondant. I. Roll out the fondant evenly with a fondant roller. J. Use the tine of a fork to make impressions on the leaf cut-outs. K. Apply luster dust for extra sparkle. L. Use a chocolate sprinkle (or chocolate vermicelli) as a stem.

SWEET COCONUT SUSHI WITH CHOCOLATE "SOY" SAUCE

YIELD: 20 pieces "sushi"

I have long admired sushi chefs for their careful presentation and skillful execution. As a sushi enthusiast, I decided to integrate their food styling techniques into a dessert. The sweet coconut rice in this dessert can be hand-formed or pressed into a *nigiri*-sushi mold. Grab extra sushi platters, decorative grass, and chopsticks from your local Japanese restaurant or sushi counter for the most realistic presentation.

The sauce is optional, but it pairs well with the sushi and makes a cute presentation.

SUSHI
- ½ cup sushi rice, medium grain, such as Nishiki
- One 14-ounce can coconut milk
- ½ cup sugar
- 20 very thin strips of dried papaya, fresh mango, or orange segments
- 5 oz. Modeling chocolate, rolled thin and cut into strips

"SOY" SAUCE
- ⅔ cup unsweetened cocoa
- 1⅔ cups sugar
- 1¼ cups water
- 1 teaspoon vanilla extract

EQUIPMENT
- *Nigiri*-sushi mold (optional)

Make the sushi rice:

1. Combine the rice, 1 cup of the coconut milk, and ¼ cup of the sugar in a medium saucepan and bring to a boil.

2. Reduce the heat to low and simmer, covered, for 20 minutes or until liquid is absorbed.

3. Remove from the heat and let cool slightly.

4. In another saucepan, boil the remaining coconut milk with the remaining ¼ cup sugar until thick and syrupy.

5. Pour the syrup over the cooled rice and cook over medium heat until thick and sticky. When it has finished cooking, there should be very little liquid remaining in the saucepan. Remove from the heat and allow the rice to cool completely.

Form the sushi:

1. When the rice cools, press spoonfuls into the *nigiri*-sushi mold cavities. If you aren't using a sushi mold, place dollops of rice (about 2 level tablespoons) on parchment and form into rectangles with your fingers. If the rice sticks to your hands, fill a small bowl with water and wet your fingertips for easier shaping.

2. Chill the shaped rice in the refrigerator for 30 minutes, or until the rice can be unmolded without sticking.

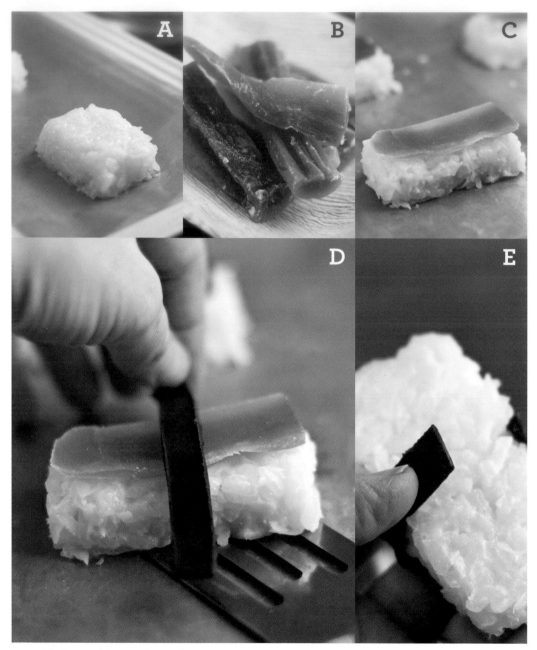

A. Mold the rice into a sushi shape. **B.** Cut strips of dried papaya to the length of the rice mounds. **C.** Lay the slices of dried papaya to mimic salmon. **D.** Use a strip of chocolate modeling clay as *nori* (the seaweed wrapped around real sushi). **E.** Fasten the chocolate clay together underneath the rice. **F.** Chocolate "soy" sauce makes a playful accompaniment.

F

not soy sauce!

3. Sliced dried papaya makes a good faux raw salmon. Trim the papaya to match the size of the rice bundles. After unmolding the rice, place the *nigiri* pieces on parchment and top with thinly sliced dried papaya.

4. As a substitute for nori (the seaweed used to wrap sushi), use chocolate modeling clay that has been rolled thin and cut into strips. You may also use soy sushi wrappers, which are mostly tasteless and come in a rainbow of colors. Press the ends of the chocolate strip together on the bottom side of the *nigiri* and

serve on sushi platters with chocolate "soy" sauce (recipe follows) on the side.

Make the "soy" sauce:

1. In a medium saucepan over medium heat, combine the cocoa, sugar, and water. Bring to a boil and let bubble for 1 minute.

2. Remove from the heat and stir in the vanilla. If not using immediately, transfer to a jar and store in the refrigerator, and heat again before serving.

TUILE COOKIE SPOONS WITH PEANUT BUTTER MOUSSE

YIELD: 50 mousse-filled spoons

While searching for unique dessert presentations, I happened upon a peanut butter mousse recipe that was served in the bowl of a teaspoon. I wasn't crazy about the idea of committing 32 pieces of flatware for a single bite, so I searched for, and found, a way to make edible spoons. And because these edible spoons are smaller than real spoons, there are even more to go around.

This recipe requires a specialty culinary stencil that can be ordered online, or you can make your own from sturdy plastic or cardboard using the template provided on page 264.

MOUSSE

⅔ cup heavy whipping cream
8-ounce package cream cheese, softened
1⅓ cups creamy peanut butter
1 cup sifted confectioners' sugar
1 teaspoon vanilla extract

TEMPLATE (see page 264)

TUILES

3 egg whites
1 cup confectioners' sugar
½ plus 2 tablespoons all-purpose flour
2 tablespoons dark cocoa powder
4 tablespoons butter, melted
1 teaspoon vanilla extract

GARNISH

Unsweetened cocoa powder for dusting
Large crystal sugar for sprinkling

Make the mousse:

1. In a small chilled mixing bowl, beat the heavy whipping cream with an electric hand mixer on medium speed until soft peaks form.

2. In another mixing bowl beat the cream cheese and peanut butter with an electric hand mixer until well incorporated.

3. Beat in the confectioners' sugar and vanilla until smooth.

4. Gently fold in the beaten whipped cream, in two additions, until the mixture is smooth. Cover and chill for 3 hours.

Make the stencil:

1. Use the template on page 264 to create the spoon stencil from a sturdy piece of cardboard or plastic large enough to accommodate the template (thin, flexible cutting mats or ice cream carton lids are ideal because they can be washed and reused).

2. Place the cardboard or plastic on a cutting board. Place the template on top and tape the edges to the cardboard or plastic.

3. Using an X-Acto knife fitted with a new blade, trace the outlines of the spoons, cutting through the template and the cardboard or plastic underneath.

4. Discard the spoon cut-outs that fall away when the stencil is picked up.

5. Make sure the stencil is neat and clean before using. If using cardboard, remove any remaining bits of paper clinging to the stencil.

Make the *tuiles*:

1. Whisk the egg whites and confectioners' sugar together until smooth.

2. Stir in the flour and cocoa powder and whisk lightly until just combined.

3. Pour in the melted butter and add a few drops of vanilla extract; stir until smooth.

4. Cover with plastic wrap and let chill in the refrigerator for 30 minutes.

5. Preheat the oven to 350°F. Grease a baking pan and line with parchment paper. Place the

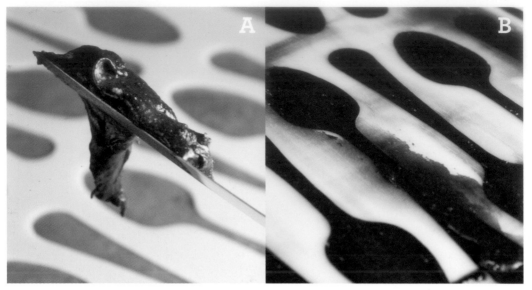

A. *Tuile* batter should be thick. Spread it into crevices with an off-set spatula. B. Spread the batter into the cookie stencil. C. Shape the spoons over a rolling pin as soon as they leave the oven.

spoon stencil on top of the parchment. Place a clean rolling pin on a nearby work surface.

6. With an offset spatula, spread *tuile* batter over the entire stencil and into the spoon crevices. Scrape off the excess with the side of the offset spatula and remove the stencil.

7. Bake the *tuiles* for 5 to 8 minutes.

8. Working very quickly, remove the *tuiles* with a spatula and place the handle portion of each spoon across the curve of the rolling pin.

Note: These cookies bake for a short time, so keep close by the oven. When done and still warm, the cookies have a rubbery texture, so they are easily shaped. Work quickly when transferring these from the oven. They harden quickly, so use the stove top or a nearby counter as a workspace. Leave the oven door open with the cookie sheet still inside while transferring the cookies from the oven to the rolling pin.

9. Allow the spoons to harden. Remove from the rolling pin and place on a serving platter.

10. Transfer the chilled peanut butter mousse to a pastry bag fitted with a large star tip.

11. Pipe a small amount of the peanut butter mousse into the bowls of 50 *tuile* spoons. Don't over-fill or the spoon handles will break when picked up.

12. Sprinkle with the cocoa powder and large-crystal sugar, and serve.

TUILE TIPS

- *Tuiles* and other cookies made from stencil paste will not harden properly in humid conditions. Do not store them in the refrigerator.

- Make these the same day you plan to serve them.

C

work
quickly
when
shaping
these!

MUSHROOM COOKIES

YIELD: Approximately 20 "mushrooms"

These mushrooms may look like they are destined for a stockpot or stew, but they are not fungi! Sweet vanilla cookie dough is rolled and hand-molded with a soda pop bottle to form these remarkable-looking cookies. Poppy seeds are added to the stems for a freshly foraged appearance. Check your craft store for fun, natural-looking papers or fibers that resemble a forest floor to display the cookies on.

---

4 tablespoons butter, softened
½ cup sugar
1 egg, at room temperature
1 teaspoon vanilla extract
1½ cups cornstarch

½ cup all-purpose flour
1 teaspoon baking powder
¼ cup unsweetened cocoa powder
Poppy seeds and corn syrup (optional)

---

1. Preheat the oven to 375°F. Line a baking sheet with parchment. Wash and dry a glass or plastic soda bottle.

2. Using a small egg whisk, cream together the butter and sugar.

3. Add the egg and vanilla extract; whisk again.

4. Add the cornstarch and mix together with your hands.

5. Gradually add the flour and baking powder. Knead the mixture with your hands and let stand for 5 minutes.

6. Roll pieces of the dough into balls between your palms. The cookies should be about the size of a walnut. Place the rolled cookies on the prepared baking sheet.

7. Place 1 tablespoon of water in a small bowl and the cocoa in another. Dip the mouth of the bottle into the water, and then dip it in the cocoa.

8. With a dough ball cupped in the palm of your hand, press the mouth of the bottle into the top of the ball. This creates the mushroom stem. Clean the mouth of the bottle every 2 to 3 uses with a paper towel.

9. Return the mushroom cookies to the baking sheet.

10. Bake for 25 minutes. Arrange the cookies on a wire rack and allow them to cool.

OPTIONAL

1. Pour the poppy seeds in a small plate.

2. Brush the ends of the cookie "stems" sparingly with corn syrup.

3. Dip the stems in the poppy seeds.

poppy seeds look like soil!

A. Bottles and cocoa powder make magic in this recipe. **B.** Coat a bottle mouth in cocoa, and press it into the cookie ball. **C.** Once sculpted, the cookies are ready for baking. **D.** Add poppy seeds to the stems for an authentic appearance.

SALTED CARAMEL CUPCAKES

YIELD: 15 cupcakes

Sculptural hard caramel gives these delicious salty-and-sweet cupcakes an elegant silhouette. Note that I use both salted and unsalted butter in the recipe; it's important because it gives the filling and icing that fantastic balance of sweet, salty, and deep caramel flavor.

BROWN SUGAR CUPCAKES

- 1½ cups all-purpose flour
- 1 teaspoon baking powder
- ¼ teaspoon sea salt
- ¼ pound (1 stick) unsalted butter, at room temperature
- 1 cup plus 2 tablespoons packed light brown sugar
- 2 eggs, at room temperature
- 1 teaspoon vanilla
- ½ cup plus 2 tablespoons buttermilk, at room temperature

SALTED CARAMEL FILLING

- ½ cup sugar
- 3 tablespoons salted butter, cubed
- ¼ cup plus 1 tablespoon heavy cream, at room temperature

SALTED CARAMEL BUTTERCREAM

- ¼ cup sugar
- 2 tablespoons water
- ¼ cup heavy cream
- 1 teaspoon vanilla extract
- ¼ pound (1 stick) salted butter, softened
- ¼ pound (1 stick) butter, softened
- ½ teaspoon sea salt
- 1½ cups confectioners' sugar

SALTED CARAMEL CANDY HALOS

- 1¼ cups granulated sugar
- ¼ teaspoon sea salt
- ¾ cup cold water
- 2 to 4 tablespoons of large-crystal decorative sugar

Make the brown sugar cupcakes:

1. Preheat the oven to 325°F. Line 2 muffin tins with paper cupcake liners.

2. Combine the flour, baking powder, and salt.

3. In the bowl of a stand mixer fitted with the paddle attachment, cream the butter and brown sugar on medium-high speed until pale and fluffy.

4. Add the eggs, one at a time, beating until each is incorporated.

5. Add the vanilla and mix. Scrape down the sides of the bowl as needed.

6. Add the flour mixture in three batches, alternating with two additions of buttermilk, and beating until combined after each.

7. Divide the batter evenly among the lined cups, filling each about halfway full.

8. Bake for approximately 25 minutes, or until a toothpick inserted in the cakes comes out clean. Transfer the cupcake pan to a wire rack

and cool for 10 minutes. Turn the cupcakes out onto racks and let cool completely.

Make the salted caramel filling:

1. Melt the sugar over medium-high heat in a large pot. Whisk the sugar as it melts, and cook until it becomes a deep amber color.

2. Add the butter and stir it in until melted.

3. Pour in the heavy cream (the mixture will foam) and whisk until the mixture becomes a smooth sauce.

Note: If lumps form, keep stirring over gentle heat until they have melted.

4. Remove from heat and let cool slightly.

5. To fill the cupcakes, cut a small round piece about 1 inch wide and 1 inch deep out of the top of each cooled cupcake and pour in 1 teaspoon of the caramel filling. Replace the cake piece.

Make the salted caramel buttercream:

1. In a saucepan, stir together the sugar and water. Bring to a boil over medium-high heat. Cook without stirring until the mixture turns a deep amber color.

2. Remove from the heat and slowly add the cream and vanilla, stirring until very smooth.

3. Let the caramel cool for about 20 minutes, until it is just barely warm and still pourable.

4. In a mixer fitted with the paddle attachment, beat the butters and salt together until lightened and fluffy.

5. Reduce the speed to low and add the confectioners' sugar. Mix until thoroughly combined.

6. Scrape down the sides of the bowl. With the motor running on low, slowly pour in the cooled caramel.

7. Beat on medium-high speed until light and airy and completely mixed, about 2 minutes.

8. Fit a large pastry bag with a large star tip; transfer the icing to the bag and decorate the cooled cupcakes with swirls of icing.

Note: The frosting should be ready to use without refrigeration. If the caramel was too hot when added, the icing will be runny. If this happens, refrigerate for 15 to 20 minutes and then rewhip with the paddle until light and fluffy.

Make the salted caramel candy halos:

1. Lay out a large piece of parchment on a work surface and spray with cooking oil. Fill the kitchen sink partially full of ice water.

2. Put the granulated sugar, salt, and water in a heavy pan; stir over low heat until the sugar dissolves. Increase the heat and bring the syrup to a boil. Lower the heat slightly and swirl the pan once or twice as the syrup caramelizes so it will color evenly; do not stir.

3. When the caramel is deep amber, plunge the base of the pan into ice water for about 2 seconds to stop further cooking.

4. Working quickly, dip a spoon in the caramel and let it fall onto the parchment paper in a drizzle. Move the spoon in a circular motion to create spirals as the syrup falls from the spoon. Repeat 15 times.

5. When the caramel spirals have cooled but are still slightly sticky, sprinkle on the large-crystal sugar. Let the caramel cool completely before peeling the halos from the paper and adorning the cupcakes.

A. Cut a small divot and fill it with caramel. **B.** Replace the cut-out cake piece. **C.** Drizzle hard caramel to create an unusual cupcake garnish. **D.** The cross-section shows exactly how these cupcakes are constructed.

HAZELNUT COFFEE MOUSSE

YIELD: 6 servings

Paired with bittersweet chocolate and hazelnuts, the coffee in this recipe imparts a truly refined flavor. My favorite element of this dessert is the gravity-defying garnish. It gives an otherwise ordinary cup of mousse wow factor.

HAZELNUT MOUSSE
- ½ cup raw hazelnuts
- 4 ounces bittersweet chocolate, chopped into pieces
- ¼ cup superfine sugar
- 1 teaspoon instant coffee
- ¼ teaspoon salt
- 1¼ cups heavy cream

CARAMELIZED HAZELNUT GARNISH
- 10 long skewers (barbecue or kebab type)
- 10 whole hazelnuts (you need only 6 for garnish, but have extra in case some break)
- 1 cup sugar
- ½ teaspoon lemon juice

Make the hazelnut mousse:

1. Preheat the oven to 375°F.

2. Spread the hazelnuts in a single layer on a jelly roll pan. Bake for 8 minutes until toasted and fragrant.

3. Pour the hazelnuts onto a clean tea towel and rub vigorously to remove as much of the hazelnut skins as possible.

4. In the bowl of a food processor, chop the hazelnuts, chocolate, sugar, coffee, and salt until fine, about 3 minutes.

5. In a small saucepan over medium heat, bring ½ cup of the heavy cream to a boil.

6. Turn the food processor on and pour the hot heavy cream through the feed tube. Process until smooth. Transfer to a bowl and let cool completely.

7. In a large bowl, whip the remaining ¾ cup cream with a handheld mixer until soft peaks form. Fold one-quarter of the whipped cream into the chocolate mixture to loosen.

8. Fold in the remaining whipped cream until just blended. Pour the mousse into espresso cups and cover with plastic wrap. Place in the refrigerator for 1 hour to firm.

Make the caramelized hazelnut garnish:

1. Fill the kitchen sink with 2 inches of cold water; add a few ice cubes to the water. Cover the floor with parchment under a table edge or countertop (the parchment will catch the drips after the skewered hazelnuts have been dipped in the caramel).

2. Carefully skewer the hazelnuts. It helps to lay them on a towel so they don't roll around while you're trying to skewer them.

A. Rub toasted hazelnuts in a tea towel while they are still warm to remove the skins. **B.** Skewer untoasted hazelnuts to ready them for dipping. **C.** Dip the skewered hazelnuts in the caramel.
D. Allow the dipped hazelnuts to harden over the edge of a table.

3. Combine the sugar and lemon juice in a saucepan. Stir until the sugar resembles wet sand. Cook over medium heat without stirring until the sugar begins to melt around the sides of the pan and the center starts to smoke.

4. Stir the sugar, and continue to heat, stirring occasionally, until the sugar is a clear, amber color.

5. Remove from the heat and place the bottom of the pan in ice water to stop the caramel from cooking further.

6. Test the caramel by placing a skewered hazelnut into the caramel and pulling it

straight up. When the caramel pulls from the hazelnut in a large thread, the caramel is ready.

7. Working quickly, dip the skewered nuts and place them on the edge of a table or counter above the prepared parchment until they dry. Use a heavy book to anchor the ends of the skewers so they don't fall off the edge of the table. Let the caramelized nuts harden completely.

8. Just before serving, carefully remove the skewers and top each cup of chilled mousse with a candied hazelnut.

ORIGAMI COOKIES

YIELD: 12 "origami" cookies

This is my sweet homage to the fascinating art of paper sculpture. The crane is an auspicious figure in Japanese culture, and it is also one of the most famous origami designs.

ORIGAMI COOKIES
- ½ pound (2 sticks) butter, softened
- 1 cup plus 2 tablespoons sugar
- 1 egg, lightly beaten
- 1 teaspoon vanilla extract
- 3 cups all-purpose flour, plus more for rolling
- Pinch of salt

TEMPLATE (see page 263)
ICING ADHESIVE
- 1 egg white
- ¾ cup confectioners' sugar
- ½ teaspoon lemon juice

Make the cookies:

1. Line a baking sheet with parchment.

2. In a mixer with a paddle attachment, mix the butter and sugar together until just incorporated. Do not over-mix at this stage, or the cookies may spread while baking.

3. Add the egg and vanilla extract. Mix again on low speed, stopping to scrape down the sides of the bowl intermittently as needed.

4. Add the flour and salt. Mix on low speed until a firm dough is formed.

5. Turn the dough out onto a sheet of plastic wrap and form into a ball. The dough will not be sticky and should be easy to work with your hands. Wrap tightly and refrigerate for 1 hour.

6. Working on a well-floured surface, knead the dough slightly, squeezing it with your hands to flatten the ball into a disc.

7. Using a floured rolling pin, roll the dough evenly to a ½-inch thickness. I suggest using rolling-pin guide bands as a guide for this project. The cookies must be rolled thickly and evenly so they will stand on their own when baked.

8. Using the template provided on page 263, cut origami pieces out of the rolled dough. Cut extra wings, as you will use them as props when drying the assembled cookies.

9. Before baking, score the cookies with the back of a knife to create "folds."

10. Transfer the scored pieces to the prepared baking sheet. Refrigerate the cutouts for 1 hour. This will help the cookies maintain a crisp shape during baking.

11. Preheat the oven to 350°F. Bake the cookies for 10 to 12 minutes or until just lightly golden and fragrant. Transfer to racks to cool completely.

Make the icing adhesive:

1. Whisk together the egg white, confectioners' sugar, and lemon juice in a small bowl. The mixture should be of piping consistency (the equivalent of stiff-peak royal icing). If the mixture is too thin, add more confectioners' sugar. If the mixture is too thick, add a little milk or water to bring to the desired consistency.

2. Transfer the mixture to a piping bag fitted with a size 1 or 2 small plain tip.

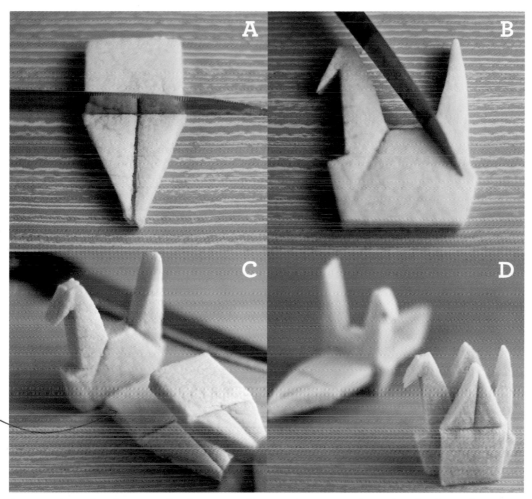

wing prop.

A. Wing: Score first horizontally, then vertically. B. Body: Score at the neck and tail. C. A spare wing can be used to prop up the iced wing. D. Arrange some cranes with their wings up and others with their wings down.

Assemble the cranes:

1. To assemble the cookies with the crane's wings up, pipe a small dot of icing on the backs of the wings (nonscored side). Press the wings against the body and lay the assembled cookie on its side to dry.

2. To assemble the cookies with the crane's wings down: With the body standing, lay a wing piece on one side of the body—do not apply icing to this piece. This is only a prop. Apply a line of icing to the bottom of the square side of a second wing piece. Gently stack the iced piece over the prop and press into the body. Repeat on the other side of the body. Allow the icing to dry completely.

3. You may also use 2 long ½-inch dowels to prop the wings on while they dry.

CLOUD MERINGUES

YIELD: 20 meringues

A palette knife seems an unlikely tool with which to paint pictures, but many artists prefer it over the paintbrush. They are highly preferred when using a technique called "impasto." Impasto painting is executed with a thick paint that is slow to dry and can be used for three-dimensional sculptural rendering right on the canvas.

In this recipe, thick meringue is painted onto parchment paper in the impasto technique. It is dried slowly in the oven and then enjoyed as a crisp cookie. These cookies are terrific served with coffee, ice cream, lemon curd, or a simple bowl of fresh fruit.

2 egg whites, at room temperature
Pinch of cream of tartar
½ cup superfine sugar
Liquid blue food coloring

1. Preheat the oven to 170°F. Line two cookie sheets with parchment paper.

2. Place the egg whites in a spotlessly clean bowl. Whip the egg whites with an electric mixer on medium speed until frothy.

3. Stop the mixer and add the cream of tartar. Start the mixer again and continue to beat the egg whites.

4. Once the egg whites form soft peaks, increase the speed to high and gradually add the sugar, a little at a time. Beat the egg whites until they are very shiny and hold stiff peaks.

5. Add one or two drops of the food coloring and mix until well combined.

6. Pick up a generous portion of meringue with the palette knife.

7. Smooth the meringue on the parchment paper, creating three-dimensional swirls and allowing a cloud shape to form organically. Repeat the process with the remaining batter.

8. Bake the meringues for 90 minutes, rotating the pans halfway through the cooking time to ensure even baking.

9. When the meringues are done, turn off the oven and let them stand in the oven for several hours or overnight. The meringues should be hard and dry to the touch and will peel easily from the parchment.

MAD HATTER MARSHMALLOW POPS

YIELD: 12 pops

We're taking another trip through the looking glass with these *Alice in Wonderland*–inspired treats. Transforming marshmallows into these Mad Hatter pops (which mimic Sir John Tenniel's original book illustrations) is simple with fondant and lollipop sticks.

LOLLIPOPS
8 ounces green fondant (see page 74)
12 large marshmallows
Corn syrup or piping gel
2 ounces orange fondant (see page 74)

EQUIPMENT
Small fondant roller
Plain-edge knife
Small artist's brush
Black food writer
12 lollipop sticks

1. Work with half of the green fondant at a time. Store the half you are not using in a zip-top bag with the air removed. With the fondant roller, roll half of the green fondant to a ¼-inch thickness.

2. Lay a marshmallow on top of the rolled fondant and cut around it with the plain-edge knife, to about ½-inch larger than the circumference of the marshmallow top.

3. Using your fingers, smooth the fondant over the top of the marshmallow and partially down the sides.

4. Cut a long length of fondant a little larger than the height of the marshmallow and evenly trim one long side. It should be large enough to completely wrap around the marshmallow. Line up the top edge of the marshmallow covered with fondant with the straight trimmed edge of the long piece.

5. Roll the piece of green fondant around the marshmallow. Cut the edges that meet on the side of the marshmallow so that they are just overlapping and perfectly vertical. Secure the edge by applying piping gel with a small artist's brush to the underside, and press at the seam to adhere.

6. Turn the marshmallow upside down and fold excess fondant toward the center of the bottom of the marshmallow. This doesn't have to be perfect, as it will be covered with another piece of fondant that will be the hat brim.

ARMATURE

Sculptors sometimes use a base to support their works called an *armature*. Armatures are the supporting core that is used to sculpt around. The supporting armature in this project is a marshmallow. It is the unseen skeleton of the finished sculpted form.

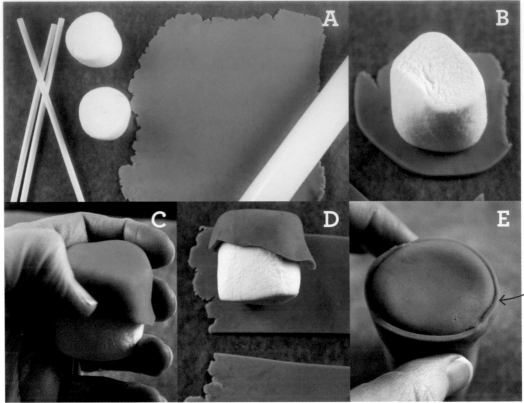

a small dab of corn syrup holds them together

A. Gather marshmallows, lollipop sticks, and rolled fondant. **B.** Place a marshmallow on a small piece of fondant. **C.** Use this piece of fondant to cover the top of the hat. **D.** Roll the marshmallow in green fondant to cover the sides. **E.** Trim the edges and press them together.

7. Using a plain-edge knife or X-Acto knife, cut an oval piece of fondant for the hat brim that is at least ¼ inch wider in circumference than the hat base.

8. Brush corn syrup over the center of the oval fondant piece, and lay it over the previously tucked fondant. Set the hat on its top (upside down) and let the hat set at room temperature for a few hours so the corn syrup can adhere well and the brim can harden.

9. To make the hatband, pinch off small pieces of orange fondant and roll them into skinny ropes. Drape around the brim of the hat and press to adhere.

10. Roll out the remaining white fondant and cut out "hat tags" approximately ½ inch by 1 inch. With a food writer, draw 10/6 on one side. To apply, brush a little corn syrup on the back of the tag and press into the side of the hat.

11. Gently press a lollipop stick through the middle of the brim and into the marshmallow, and turn right-side up.

12. The pops can be decoratively packaged in cellophane bags and tied with a ribbon.

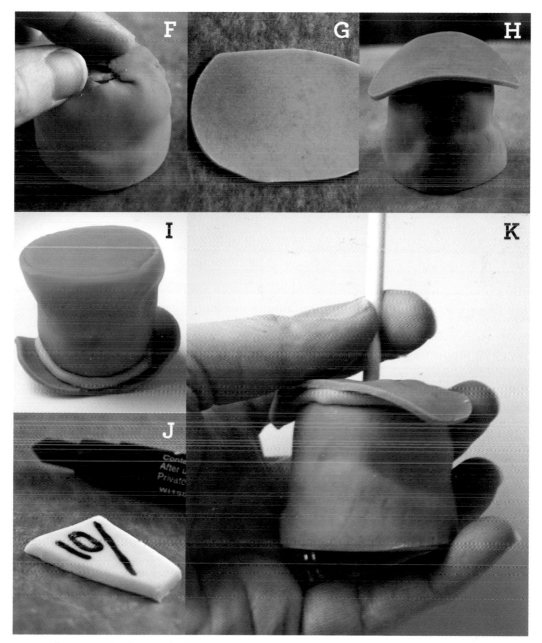

F. Trim the excess fondant at the bottom and pinch it together. **G.** Cut a small oval piece of fondant for the brim of the hat. **H.** Use a dot of corn syrup to glue the fondant brim in place. **I.** Add a colorful hat band. **J.** Use a food writer to make the price ticket. **K.** Insert a lollipop stick into the hat and through the marshmallow.

COLOR

Color is a powerful component of dessert composition. We eat with our eyes first, and upon seeing the deep red color of wine-poached pears or the grassy green of matcha tea cake, the brain starts sending information to your taste buds before you've taken the first bite. Whenever possible, I like to use naturally derived food colorings from a variety of sources. Berries, teas, seeds, root vegetables, and wines are all favorite color-yielding ingredients. But I'm not a purist— I use food-safe artificial colorings, too.

COLOR WHEEL

The color wheel is a tool used for mixing colors and creating harmonious color combinations. It also shows the relationships between colors. The most common color wheel has 12 colors based on the colors red, yellow, and blue. There are many fundamental lessons to learn from the color wheel, and we'll begin with color mixing.

The three *primary colors* are red, blue and yellow.

Mixing two of these colors in equal parts will create *secondary colors*; they are purple, green, and orange.

Tertiary colors are the mixture of equal parts primary color and its secondary color. Browns and grays are also commonly referred to as tertiary colors, as they are made by mixing together primary colors.

Shade, Tint, and Hue

We've all contemplated our favorite shade or hue, but many don't realize that those words have completely different meanings.

- *Shade* is a color mixed with black, which decreases lightness. For example, dark blue can be created by combining royal blue and black.

- *Tint* is a color mixed with white. It increases lightness. Most plain icings are white; therefore, you may already have plenty of experience with tinting! For example, royal blue food coloring mixed with white icing will yield a lighter tint of blue.

- *Hue* is the color itself, in its pure form: blue, yellow, green, orange—whatever base color you are working with. It is without tint or shade.

COLOR HARMONY

Harmonious color is an arrangement of colors that is aesthetically pleasing. Color schemes consist of two or more colors with a fixed relation on the color wheel. Here are some examples of common and easy-to-use schemes.

Adjacent color schemes are a combination of colors that are right next to each other on the color wheel. They flow together harmoniously and are very pleasing to the eye. This is a good scheme for beginners to practice when decorating cakes and confections.

Two Primary Colors

When using two primary colors, use less of one than the other to create a harmonious color balance.

Monochromatic Color Scheme

A monochromatic color scheme is a collection of different tints and shades of one hue. Use this scheme to tint cake layers and in other layer applications.

Warm color tones are reds, yellows, and oranges, which are often associated with heat and energy.

Cool colors are blues, greens, and violets, often associated with ice and calmness, or serenity.

NATURAL HUES

Wines, root vegetables, teas, berries, and other fruits can be used to create beautiful color on the plate.

- **Strawberries, blackberries, raspberries:** These berries are at their most brilliant when pureed. Use the puree in icings or as a berry coulis.

- **Matcha tea:** Unlike fruits, matcha tea can be baked without losing any of its glorious grassy color. Use it in cakes, breads, and other baked goods.

- **Wine:** Red and rosé wines can be used to impart rouge tones to poached fruits and reductions.

- **Root vegetables:** Sweet potatoes yield warm orange and striking purple hues. Ube (purple yam) can be found at Asian markets in the produce section or pureed and canned. Both hold their color well in pies but less so in confections with a large ratio of flour such as cakes and muffins.

A. *Crème* candy dough is tinted in graduating intensities with red gel food coloring. **B.** Reds and oranges surround a pumpkin cake with warm, fragrant spices. **C.** Use color to reflect flavor profiles in the confections you create. Cool mint green suggests the minty flavor of grasshopper pie.

COLORED ICINGS
AND BATTERS

Mixing colors is easy and practical, and as long as you have the three primary colors along with black and white, you will be able to create most any color you need. Black and white cannot be achieved by mixing the three primary colors.

Before blending colors together to make new ones, you must first know how to mix colors into icing and batter. Keep the following tips in mind:

• I use and recommend gel food colorings for tinting icing. Gel colorings are concentrated and won't change the icing's consistency.

• Add small amounts of gel color at a time. Dip color from the bottle and then into the icing or batter with a toothpick. Use a new toothpick for each addition.

• For intense color, use gel food coloring in larger amounts. Retrieve gel food coloring in dime-size portions using an offset spatula. Repeat as needed, cleaning the spatula after each addition.

• Cake batter and cookie dough are already tinted slightly yellow from egg yolks and butter. Both require larger amounts of food coloring than icing does to achieve a desired color.

• Blend the icing or batter and gel colors together gently using a rubber spatula. This is especially important when tinting cake batter; overbeating adversely affects the texture of the finished cake

COLOR WHEEL CUPCAKES

YIELD: Approximately 20 cupcakes

This exercise will teach you the basics of color mixing. While mixing your own color wheel of cupcakes, use the color wheel as a guide while following the recipe instructions.

CUPCAKES

- ¼ pound (1 stick) butter, softened
- 1 cup sugar
- 1 egg, at room temperature
- 2 teaspoons vanilla extract
- 1½ cups all-purpose flour
- 2 teaspoons baking powder
- ½ teaspoon salt
- 1 cup buttermilk, at room temperature

SWISS BUTTERCREAM

- 1 cup sugar
- 3 egg whites
- ¾ pound (3 sticks) butter, at room temperature
- 1 teaspoon pure vanilla extract
- 1 small bottle (1 ounce) red gel food coloring
- 1 small bottle (1 ounce) blue gel food coloring
- 1 small bottle (1 ounce) yellow gel food coloring

Make the cupcakes:

1. Preheat the oven to 350°F. Line 2 standard cupcake pans with paper cupcake liners.

2. Combine the butter and sugar in the bowl of a stand mixer fitted with the paddle attachment. Beat on medium-high speed until light and fluffy.

3. Beat in the egg and vanilla extract.

4. Whisk together the flour, baking powder, and salt.

5. Add the flour mixture and buttermilk to the sugar mixture alternately in 3 batches, beginning and ending with the flour mixture and scraping down the bowl between additions.

6. Fill the cupcake liners halfway with the batter. Bake for 15 to 20 minutes, until a toothpick inserted in the center of a cupcake comes out clean.

7. Cool in the pan for 5 minutes. Turn onto a rack to cool completely before icing.

Make the Swiss buttercream:

1. Set a medium saucepan one-quarter full of water over medium heat and bring to a simmer.

2. Whisk together the sugar and egg whites in a heatproof mixing bowl.

3. Set the bowl over the simmering water and whisk constantly until the sugar has melted. Cook until the mixture feels hot to the touch.

4. Remove the bowl from the top of the saucepan, wipe the bottom with a towel, and transfer the contents to the bowl of a stand mixer fitted with the whisk attachment.

5. Beat on medium-high speed until the mixture has doubled in size and has cooled, about

10 minutes. The mixer bowl should feel cool to the touch.

6. Switch to the paddle attachment and turn the mixer on medium-low. Add the butter 1 tablespoon at a time, beating well after each addition.

7. Add the vanilla and beat again until it is completely incorporated and the icing is fluffy.

8. To mix the colors, in three separate bowls, divide the icing evenly and mix each primary color with the icing: 1 blue, 1 yellow, 1 red. Mixing icing color is different from mixing paint because each food coloring is blended with white frosting and not a singular pigment. White lightens pigment, so add a large amount of food coloring to each frosting bowl. It's a good idea to dedicate an entire 1-ounce bottle of each primary coloring for this project.

9. After each color is mixed, frost 3 cupcakes with about ½ cup of each color and place them in a triangle on your work surface. Place the yellow at the top, the blue to the bottom left, and the red to the bottom right.

10. In another bowl, mix equal parts (2 or 3 tablespoons each) of yellow and red icing to make orange. Frost a cupcake with the orange icing and place it between the yellow and red cupcakes.

11. In yet another bowl, mix equal parts (2 to 3 tablespoons each) yellow and blue icing to make green. Frost a cupcake with the green icing and place it between the yellow and blue cupcakes.

12. In still another bowl, mix equal parts red and blue (2 to 3 tablespoons each) to make purple (or violet). Frost a cupcake with the purple icing and set it between the red and blue cupcakes. These are your secondary colors.

Note: Tertiary colors are created by mixing a primary color with its "offspring." You may need to mix more secondary colors (orange, green, and purple) to produce tertiary colors.

13. Mix equal parts of red and orange icing to make red-orange icing. Frost a cupcake and place it between the red and orange cupcakes.

14. Continue this process with red and violet to make violet-red; blue and violet to make blue-violet; blue and green to make blue-green; green and yellow to make yellow-green; and yellow and orange to make yellow-orange.

Your color wheel is now complete.

You may have leftover icing and a few extra cupcakes. Frost the extra cupcakes and enjoy!

BLACKBERRY CURD

YIELD: about 2 cups

Blackberry curd is a perfect example of how natural hues can be bold and beautiful. Black-berries impart a deep magenta color in this curd and rich flavor that will have you sampling it straight from the jar. Use it on sponge cakes (see *Genoise* Sponge Cake on page 40), biscuits, toast, cookies—everything.

1½ cups blackberries
¼ cup water
¼ cup sugar
3 egg yolks
6 tablespoons cold butter, cut into pats

1. Purée the blackberries with the water using a blender or food processor.

2. Set a sieve over a small saucepan and strain the puree to remove the seeds.

3. Place the saucepan over medium heat and add the sugar. Stir until dissolved.

4. Bring to a simmer, and cook for 10 minutes, stirring occasionally.

5. Lower the heat. With a wire whisk, quickly stir in 1 of the egg yolks. Whisk briskly, so as to not turn the yolk into scrambled eggs. Add the second yolk, then the third, whisking constantly.

6. Cook for 10 to 15 more minutes over low heat, whisking occasionally, until the mixture is thick and begins to bubble.

7. Remove from the heat and stir in the butter pats one at a time, adding the next after the previous has melted.

8. Use immediately over plain cake (such as sponge or pound cake), or chill in the refrigerator until set.

INSPIRATION

Perhaps the best advice I can give you regarding color is to keep your eyes open at all times for inspiring examples in real life. It could be a frilly pink prom dress or a plaid shirt, a robin's egg, or autumn leaves. Then think of ways to implement those hues in your baking and decorating to tell your own story in glorious color.

BLUE VELVET CUPCAKES

YIELD: 24 cupcakes

Working with food coloring is different from working with an artist's box of acrylics or watercolors. When trying to achieve a specific color, you must take into account natural colors that exist in the cake batter or cookie dough you are working with. Bright yellow egg yolks and even pale yellow butter can derail a specific color plan.

The color wheel tells us that yellow and blue make green, and that's exactly what color cupcakes you'll get by adding blue food coloring to this recipe. Another color must be added to counter (or color-correct) the yellow in the batter. Mixing complementary colors together decreases the intensity of both colors. The complementary color of yellow is purple, so a dab of purple food coloring will remedy this problem.

This batter can also yield a navy blue shade if a small amount of black food coloring is added to the finished batter.

CUPCAKES
- ½ pound (2 sticks) butter, softened
- 2 cups sugar
- 2 eggs, at room temperature
- 1 tablespoon cocoa powder
- ½ to 1 tablespoon royal blue gel food coloring
- 2½ cups all-purpose flour
- 1 teaspoon salt
- 1 cup buttermilk, at room temperature
- 1 teaspoon vanilla extract
- 1 tablespoon vinegar
- ½ teaspoon baking soda
- 1 small dab of black or violet gel food coloring (dip a toothpick in the container and use that much)

CREAM CHEESE FROSTING
- 1 pound cream cheese, softened
- ½ pound (2 sticks) butter, softened
- 1 teaspoon vanilla extract
- 4 cups sifted confectioners' sugar

Make the cupcakes:

1. Preheat the oven to 350°F. Prepare cupcake pans with paper liners.

2. In a mixing bowl with a handheld mixer or in the bowl of a stand mixer fitted with the paddle attachment, cream the butter and sugar; mix until fluffy.

3. Add the eggs 1 at a time, mixing well after each addition.

4. In a small bowl, mix the cocoa powder and blue food coloring together to form a paste. Add to the butter-sugar mixture and beat to combine.

5. Combine the flour and salt. Add to the blue mixture alternately with the buttermilk in 3 batches, beginning and ending with the flour.

6. Add the vanilla extract and mix.

7. Combine the vinegar and baking soda in a small bowl. Add to the batter. The mixture will bubble and foam. Mix well.

8. Dip a toothpick in the violet gel food coloring, add it to the batter, and mix again until a uniform color has developed.

9. Pour the batter into the cupcake papers, filling each cup halfway. The batter will be very thick.

10. Bake for 25 to 30 minutes, or until a toothpick inserted into the center of a cupcake comes out clean. Remove from the oven, transfer to a wire rack, and let cool completely before frosting.

Make the cream cheese frosting:
1. In a large mixing bowl, beat the cream cheese, butter, and vanilla together until smooth.

2. Add the sugar and beat on low speed until incorporated. Increase the speed to high and mix until very light and fluffy.

3. Reserve four baked cupcakes for embellishment purposes. Frost the remaining cupcakes with a butter knife, or pipe the frosting on with a large star tip.

4. To embellish the cupcakes, slice the reserved uniced cupcakes vertically into ¼-inch-thick pieces.

5. Working on a cutting board, press the slices flat with the palm of your hand until they become firm.

6. Use a mini-cookie cutter to cut decorative shapes for embellishment.

A. and B. Use a small cookie cutter or a large decorator tip to make embellishments.

COLORFUL SPIRAL COOKIES

YIELD: 30 cookies

The use of bright colors in this recipe communicates a feeling of cheerfulness and energy. They are easily made in a food processor, and the dough can be kept in the freezer for slice-and-bake convenience.

- 2 cups plus 2 tablespoons all-purpose flour
- ½ teaspoon baking powder
- ¼ teaspoon salt
- ⅔ cup confectioners' sugar
- ¼ cup granulated sugar
- ½ pound plus 4 tablespoons (2½ sticks) butter, cut into pieces and kept very cold

- 1 teaspoon vanilla extract
- ½ teaspoon clear flavoring extract, such as peppermint, orange, lemon, or clear vanilla
- ½ teaspoon rose (or other) gel food coloring
- 1½ cups jumbo multicolored non-pareils

---

1. Combine 2 cups of the flour with the baking powder, salt, and sugars in a food processor, and pulse briefly to mix.

2. Add the cold butter in pieces; process with short bursts until the mixture has a crumbly consistency.

3. Add the vanilla extract and process in 3-second pulses until a dough ball forms.

4. Divide the dough in half and return one portion to the food processor. Add the clear flavor extract, gel food coloring, and the remaining 2 tablespoons of the flour to the processor and process until just incorporated.

5. Roll out each portion of dough between sheets of wax paper to form a rectangle about 11 x 8½ inches x ⅛ inch thick.

6. Transfer the rolled dough inside the wax paper onto a large cookie sheet. Refrigerate until firm, at least 2 hours.

7. Remove the dough pieces from the refrigerator.

8. Pour the nonpareil decors into a shallow rectangular dish, such as a standard 9 x 13-inch pan.

9. Peel off the top sheet of wax paper from both pieces of dough.

10. Using a pastry brush, lightly coat the vanilla dough with water.

11. Using the wax paper, lift the red dough and flip it over onto the vanilla dough so they are stacked. Gently press the two dough pieces together.

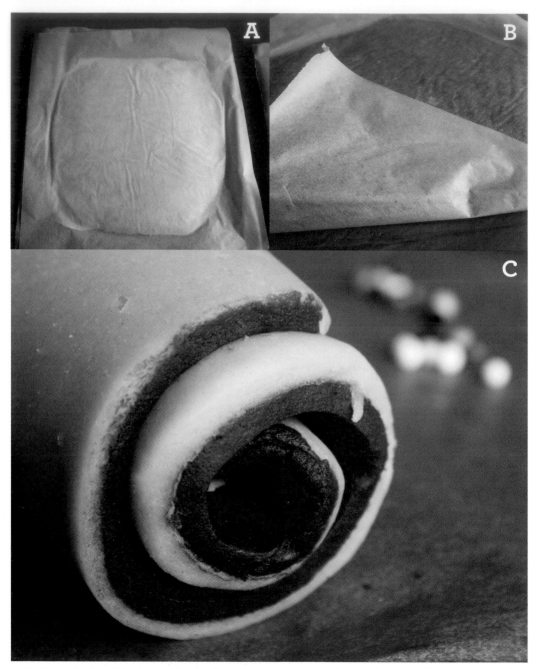

A. Roll out the dough between sheets of parchment paper. **B.** The parchment will peel away easily from thoroughly chilled dough. **C.** Tightly roll the layered dough together. **D.** Add a thorough coating of jumbo sprinkles to the dough.

12. Remove the top sheet of wax paper and trim the edges of the dough square.

13. When the dough is just pliable but still cold, roll it up along the longest side like a jelly roll.

14. Gently curl the edge with your fingertips so you don't get any air pockets as you roll the dough into a log. While rolling the dough, the vanilla portion (which will be on the outside of the roll) may want to tear; pinch tears together as they happen and keep rolling.

15. After forming the dough into a log, dispose of the wax paper.

16. Gently lift the log and place it on top of the nonpareils in the dish. Roll until the log is completely coated with sprinkles.

17. Wrap the log in plastic wrap and refrigerate until firm enough to slice, about 3 hours.

Note: Cookie dough can be frozen for up to 2 months. Defrost in the refrigerator until soft enough to slice.

18. Preheat the oven to 325°F. Line 2 baking sheets with parchment paper.

19. Slice the dough into ¼-inch-thick cookies, cutting carefully and avoiding the nonpareils, and bake on parchment-lined baking sheets for 15 to 17 minutes.

20. When done, cookies should no longer be shiny on top and the bottoms should be lightly browned.

MATCHA *GÉNOISE* LAYER CAKE

YIELD: 6 to 8 servings

For those who are wary of the bitterness of green tea, let me reassure you—this cake has none of that! Mild green tea and almond flour make for an interesting flavor combination, and the naturally grassy green color of the matcha powder makes it a pleasure to plate.

GREEN TEA *GÉNOISE*
- 2 eggs, at room temperature
- ½ cup confectioners' sugar
- ½ cup almond flour
- 1½ teaspoons matcha green tea powder
- 2 egg whites, at room temperature
- ⅛ teaspoon cream of tartar
- 2 tablespoons granulated sugar
- 2 tablespoons all-purpose flour

CRÈME FILLING
- 1 cup heavy cream
- ¼ cup sugar

WHITE CHOCOLATE MATCHA GANACHE
- ½ cup white chocolate chips
- 1 tablespoon heavy cream
- ¼ teaspoon matcha green tea powder

CANDY ALMOND GARNISH
- 6 to 8 white Jordan almonds or yogurt-covered almonds
- Extra matcha powder for sprinkling

Make the green tea *génoise*:

1. Preheat the oven to 425°F. Grease an 11 x 17-inch (or 12 x 16-inch) sheet pan with shortening. Line with parchment paper and grease the parchment.

2. Combine the eggs, confectioners' sugar, and almond flour in a bowl. Whip with a handheld mixer until the batter has lightened considerably in color.

3. Add the matcha powder and mix on low speed until combined. Set aside.

4. Whip the egg whites in a clean bowl on low speed until they are frothy.

5. Add the cream of tartar and increase the mixer speed, whipping until stiff peaks form.

6. Add the sugar and whip for a few seconds longer to incorporate.

7. Sift the all-purpose flour over the pale yellow egg mixture, and then scoop about one-third of the egg whites into the egg mixture and fold together gently with a rubber spatula. Add the remaining egg whites and fold in until uniformly mixed.

8. Pour the batter into the sheet pan and distribute it evenly with an offset spatula, making the layer as level and smooth as possible. The batter will be spread very thin.

9. Bake for 5 to 8 minutes, until the cake is just firm. Keep an eye on the cake as it bakes! It will burn easily.

10. Remove the cake from the oven and turn it out onto a cooling rack. Remove the parchment Allow the cake to cool slightly. Cut the cake into four perfectly even rectangular pieces.

Make the *crème* filling:

1. Whip the heavy cream until slightly thickened.

2. Gradually add the sugar, and whip until stiff peaks are formed.

3. Spread three cake layers with the whipped cream mixture, and stack. Top with the plain layer.

4. Chill for 1 hour.

Make the white chocolate matcha ganache:

1. Melt the white chocolate and heavy cream together—either in a saucepan over low heat or in the microwave at full power for about 30 seconds.

2. Add the matcha powder and stir until combined.

3. Remove the cake from the refrigerator and slice into 6 to 8 slices. Frost the slices with the white chocolate ganache using an offset spatula, saving a couple of tablespoons for garnish.

Prepare the candy almond garnish:

1. Dip the almonds halfway into the reserved ganache and top the cake slices.

2. Sprinkle the slices with extra matcha powder and serve.

NEAPOLITAN CAKE

YIELD: Serves 10 to 12

The classic combination of chocolate, vanilla, and strawberry doesn't have to be limited to ice cream. Delectable layers representative of the ice cream trio are brought together in cake form with a generous helping of cream cheese icing. Guests will be pleasantly surprised to find that this seemingly plain frosted cake has an eye-popping interior.

NEAPOLITAN CAKE

- ¾ pound (3 sticks) butter or 1½ cups margarine, softened
- 3 cups sugar
- 6 cups cake flour, sifted
- 2 tablespoons baking powder
- 12 egg whites, at room temperature
- 2 cups milk, at room temperature
- 1 teaspoon vanilla extract
- ½ cup hot water
- 3-ounce package strawberry-flavored powdered gelatin
- ¼ cup unsweetened cocoa powder

ICING

- 1 pound cream cheese, softened
- ½ pound (2 sticks) butter, softened
- 1 teaspoon vanilla
- 1 pound (4 cups) confectioners' sugar

CANDY CURLS

- ½ cup semisweet chocolate chips
- ½ cup strawberry candy melts

Make the cakes:

1. Preheat the oven to 325°F. Grease three 9-inch round pans and line the bottoms with parchment paper. Grease the parchment.

2. In the bowl of a stand mixer fitted with the paddle attachment, cream the butter and sugar together until light and fluffy.

3. Sift together the flour and baking powder.

4. With a handheld electric mixer, beat the egg whites until stiff peaks form—do not overbeat! The egg whites should hold peaks but not be dry.

5. With a stand mixer on low speed, add the flour mixture and milk alternately to butter mixture in 3 additions, beginning and ending with the flour mixture.

6. Gently fold the egg whites and vanilla extract into batter.

7. Divide the batter into 3 equal parts in separate bowls—about 3½ cups for each bowl. One portion will remain white. Pour the white batter into one of the prepared pans.

8. Mix ¼ cup of the hot water and the strawberry gelatin together in a small bowl. Stir until the gelatin is almost dissolved. It is okay if a few grains of gelatin remain. Pour the gelatin mixture into a bowl of batter and mix until consistently pink. Pour into the second prepared pan.

9. Mix the cocoa powder and remaining ¼ cup hot water until dissolved. Combine with the remaining batter and mix until no white streaks remain. Pour into the third prepared pan.

10. Bake the cakes for 30 to 35 minutes, or until a toothpick inserted in the center comes out clean.

Note: Check the chocolate layer at 25 minutes. It bakes more quickly than the other layers because of the added cocoa powder.

11. Cool the cakes in the pans for 10 minutes; then invert and cool completely on racks.

12. Level the cakes with a serrated knife or cake leveler.

Make the icing:
1. With a hand mixer in a large mixing bowl, beat the cream cheese, butter, and vanilla together until smooth.

2. With the mixer on low, gradually pour in the confectioners' sugar and mix until incorporated.

3. Increase the speed to high and beat until light and fluffy. If the mixture is too thick, add a little milk to loosen it. If it is too thin, add additional confectioners' sugar or put in the refrigerator to firm up.

4. Frost and stack the cake layers; frost the entire cake using a large offset spatula.

Make the candy curls:
1. Melt the chocolate in the microwave at full power in 30-second intervals until smooth. Mix well between intervals to avoid overheating.

2. Spread the chocolate over a large unlined cookie sheet with an offset spatula.

3. Chill in the refrigerator until firm.

4. Remove from the refrigerator and let stand until the chocolate is at room temperature.

5. Run a small sharp-edged spatula under the chocolate, allowing the chocolate to curl forward. If the chocolate cracks rather than curls, it may still be cold. Let stand until softer and pliable.

6. Repeat the melting, spreading, chilling, and curling process with the strawberry candy melts.

7. Garnish the cake with candy curls.

use a spatula with a sharp edge

A. Combine the cocoa mixture with white cake batter. **B.** Combine the strawberry mixture with white cake batter. **C.** Level the layers and stack them. **D.** Spread melted chocolate directly on an ungreased baking sheet. **E.** Use a spatula to scrape the chocolate into curls.

MANGO AND YOGURT *GELÉES*

YIELD: 6 (½-cup) servings

I marvel at the vibrant yellow color that occurs naturally in a sweet, ripe mango. Here the fruit is pureed and topped with sweetened yogurt. Raspberries heighten the color composition by providing a sharp contrast between two primary colors.

MANGO PUREE
- 2 medium ripe mangoes
- 1 teaspoon lemon juice
- 2 tablespoons sugar (optional)

YOGURT *GELÉE*
- 2 tablespoons water
- 1½ teaspoons unflavored powdered gelatin
- 2 cups vanilla Greek yogurt
- ¼ cup superfine sugar

MERINGUE KISSES
- 2 egg whites, at room temperature
- ¼ teaspoon cream of tartar
- ½ cup superfine sugar
- Colorful sanding sugar for sprinkling (optional)
- ½ pint fresh raspberries (optional)

Make the mango puree:

1. Peel the mangoes and cut into large pieces.

2. Pour the lemon juice over the mango pieces and puree in a food processor or blender. Taste; if the mixture is too tart, add sugar if desired.

3. Pour the puree evenly into 6 (4-ounce) glasses. Place the glasses in the freezer.

Make the yogurt *gelée*:

1. Pour the water into a small bowl. Sprinkle the gelatin over the water to bloom.

2. Combine the yogurt and sugar in a saucepan, and stir to combine. Gently heat the yogurt mixture over low heat until it thins somewhat. Remove from the stovetop.

3. Microwave the gelatin for 10 seconds (it will turn to liquid) and combine with the yogurt mixture; let it cool slightly.

4. Remove the glasses from the freezer and layer the yogurt mixture on top of the mango puree. Refrigerate for 2 hours before serving.

Make the meringue kisses:

1. Preheat the oven to 200°F. Line 2 baking sheets with parchment paper.

2. Beat the egg whites on medium speed with an electric mixer until frothy.

3. Add the cream of tartar. Beat on high speed, adding the sugar 1 tablespoon at a time until stiff peaks form.

4. Transfer the meringue to a pastry bag fitted with a large closed star tip.

5. Pipe kisses onto prepared baking sheets.

6. Sprinkle with colorful sanding sugar.

7. Bake for 45 minutes, rotate the baking sheets, and bake for an additional 45 minutes (90 minutes total).

8. Allow the kisses to cool before removing from the pan. Store extras in an airtight container.

9. Garnish each glass of *gelées* with 2 or 3 raspberries and a meringue kiss.

SPICED WINE–POACHED PEARS

YIELD: 4 servings

One of my favorite desserts to make when it's cold outside is poached pears. This version is made with warm, fragrant spices and red wine. Adding sliced fresh beets to the simmering pot yields a poached pear with a ruby-red color. If you happen to be beet-o-phobic (I know some who are) you'll be glad to know that the beet flavor is practically undetectable—so simmer away!

4 Bosc, Bartlett, or Anjou pears
1 bottle Shiraz (or other full-bodied red) wine
1 small beet, peeled and sliced
1 cup sugar
1 vanilla bean, cut in half lengthwise

1 lemon, cut in half
2 whole cinnamon sticks
1 teaspoon ground allspice
15 (or a handful) whole cardamom pods

1. Peel the pears, leaving the stems intact, and place in a medium saucepan. Add the wine, beet, sugar, vanilla, lemon, and spices to the pan. Add just enough water to cover the pears.

2. Set the saucepan over high heat, and bring the liquid to a boil.

3. Reduce to a simmer, and cook, occasionally stirring gently, over medium-low heat, until a paring knife easily pierces the pears, 15 to 20 minutes. Remove the pan from the heat; let the pears cool in the liquid.

4. Using a slotted spoon, transfer the pears to a serving platter. With the same spoon, discard the solids from the wine mixture.

5. Return the liquid to a boil. Simmer over medium-high heat, and cook until the liquid has been reduced to a syrup, about 30 minutes.

6. Let cool; store the pears in an airtight container until ready to serve.

7. When ready to serve, arrange the pears on a platter or on individual plates, and drizzle the reduced poaching liquid over them.

SNOW APPLES

YIELD: 6 to 8 candy apples

I love the peacefulness that snow brings in the wintertime. It blankets the world in white and makes the world look fresh and clean. These marshmallow candy–coated apples reflect my love for winter's achromatic landscape.

A single primary color provides a striking contrast and makes these apples festive for Christmas. Serve them on a plate of sparkling crystal sugar. They will last 2 to 3 days at room temperature.

SNOW APPLES

6 to 8 small crisp unblemished apples, stems removed

½ cup light corn syrup

3 cups sugar

1 cup water

1 dram bottle (¾ teaspoon) marshmallow candy-flavoring oil

2 tablespoons white food coloring

Edible glitter (such as Disco Dust) for garnish (optional)

EQUIPMENT

Sturdy plastic candy canes

---

1. Grease a jelly roll pan with vegetable shortening.

2. Wash and dry the apples thoroughly and remove the stems.

3. Insert the candy canes firmly but carefully into the tops of the fruit where the stems used to be and lift to make sure each can be picked up securely without falling off.

4. Combine the corn syrup, sugar, and water in a medium saucepan with a handle. Clip a candy thermometer to the edge of the saucepan. Place the saucepan over medium-high heat and cook until the sugar has dissolved.

5. Increase the heat and bring the mixture to a boil. The sugar mixture will take 20 to 25 minutes to reach 302°F on the candy thermometer. This is known as the hard-crack stage.

6. Once the temperature has been reached, remove the pan from the burner and add the flavoring. The mixture will bubble. Mix well.

7. Quickly add the white food coloring. The mixture will bubble and sputter with this addition. Stir until a consistent color develops.

8. Dip the apples into the syrup one at a time, swirling until completely coated in syrup. Hold the fruit above the saucepan to let the excess candy drain off. As you work, you may need to tilt the saucepan to pool the candy to one side. This will help ensure that the entire surface of the fruit gets a full coating as the syrup level gets lower.

9. Place the fruit on the prepared sheet pan and allow them to harden.

10. Dust with edible glitter if desired.

GRASSHOPPER PIE

YIELD: 1 (9-inch) pie or 6 (3-inch) individual pies

This pie, a southern favorite for generations, is a take on the vintage grasshopper cocktail that was hugely popular in the fifties and sixties. The same green *crème de menthe* used in the cocktail is what gives this pie its cool mint green color.

CRUST
- 1½ cups chocolate cookie crumbs, such as crushed Nabisco Famous Wafers
- 5 tablespoons butter, melted

FILLING
- 1 cup heavy whipping cream
- 25 large marshmallows

- 2 tablespoons green *crème de menthe*
- 1 tablespoon *crème de cacao*

WHIPPED *CRÈME* TOPPING
- 1 cup heavy whipping cream
- 5 tablespoons superfine sugar
- Cocoa powder for dusting

Make the crust:

1. In a small bowl, stir together the cookie crumbs and butter.

2. If using pastry rings (as pictured), place each ring atop a piece of plastic wrap and divide the crumb mixture evenly among the rings; press firmly. If using a 9-inch pie pan, press firmly into the bottom of the pan.

Make the filling:

1. Whip the cream until stiff peaks form.

2. Microwave the marshmallows in a large heatproof bowl for 45 seconds, or until they have puffed up considerably. Remove from the microwave and stir until the marshmallows have melted and completely lost their original shape.

3. Stir the green *crème de menthe* and *crème de cacao* into the marshmallow until the mixture is smooth and uniformly green. If the mixture is warm, let it stand until it reaches room temperature.

4. Fold the whipped cream into the marshmallow mixture. The color will lighten to a pretty pale green as you mix.

5. When the whipped cream is completely incorporated, evenly spoon the mixture over the crust and smooth the top with an offset spatula. Refrigerate until set (about 1 hour).

Note: If using tart rings, freeze for easy unmolding and allow to thaw in the refrigerator before serving.

Make the whipped crème topping:

1. Place the heavy cream in a large bowl and beat with a hand mixer until soft peaks form.

2. Gradually add the sugar and whip until stiff peaks form.

3. Transfer to a pastry bag fitted with a small closed star tip and pipe onto the pie.

4. Lightly dust with cocoa powder.

A. Pour the cookie crust mixture into pastry rings. **B.** Use a glass to press the crust until it is firm.
C. Add the pie filling and cover the ring in plastic wrap for freezing.

MATCHA WHITE CHOCOLATE CHEESECAKE

YIELD: 8 to 10 servings

I use matcha tea powder often in cakes and cookies as a natural food coloring and for subtle tea flavor. It is rich in antioxidants, so it's good for you, too! Here, white chocolate pairs beautifully with matcha tea in a cold, creamy, no-bake cheesecake.

ALMOND CRUST
- ⅔ cup all-purpose flour
- ⅔ cup almond flour
- 1 teaspoon ground cinnamon
- ¼ cup sugar
- Pinch of salt
- 4 tablespoons cold butter, cut into pieces

CHEESECAKE FILLING
- 2 cups white chocolate chips
- 1 pound cream cheese at room temperature
- 1 (14-ounce) can sweetened condensed milk
- ⅔ cup water
- 1 (¼-ounce) packet unflavored powdered gelatin
- 1 cup heavy cream
- 2 tablespoons matcha green tea powder plus 1 teaspoon for dusting

Make the almond crust:

1. Preheat the oven to 350°F.

2. In a food processor, pulse the all-purpose and almond flours, cinnamon, sugar, salt, and butter until the mixture resembles coarse sand.

3. Press into the bottom (not up the sides) of a 9-inch springform pan. Bake for 10 minutes, and let cool completely.

Make the cheesecake filling:

1. In a large heatproof bowl, melt the white chocolate at 30-second intervals in the microwave at full power, stirring well after each heating.

2. When chocolate is smooth, add the cream cheese and mix well with an electric mixer.

3. Add the sweetened condensed milk and beat until smooth.

4. In a small saucepan, combine the water and gelatin. Let set for 1 minute. Heat on the stovetop on low until the gelatin has dissolved.

5. Stir gelatin into the cream cheese mixture.

6. In a separate bowl, combine (but don't whip) the heavy cream and 2 tablespoons of the matcha powder with a handheld mixer on the lowest speed until just incorporated. Fold whipped cream into cheese mixture.

7. Pour the batter over the crust and refrigerate for 4 hours.

8. To unmold the cheesecake, run a knife along the edge of the cake and pop open the springform pan. Remove the cheesecake from the mold and top with a disposable doily.

9. Put the remaining 1 teaspoon of matcha powder in a small handheld sieve and sprinkle over the doily. Carefully remove doily.

A. Place a paper doily on top of the cheesecake. Put a small amount of matcha powder in a sieve. **B.** Dust the top of the cheesecake with the Matcha powder. **C.** Remove the doily to reveal the beautiful, lacy design.

MENDIANTS

YIELD: 70 candies

Mendiant candies are small discs of tempered chocolate studded with dried fruits and nuts. Their name is related to the religious mendicant order known for giving away their earthly belongings to rely on charity for income. *Mendiant* candies are made to look like coins, representing the monies procured from handouts and begging.

The original fruits and nuts used in these candies were almonds, hazelnuts, figs, and raisins. They symbolized the colors of the robes worn by the four major mendicant orders of the Roman Catholic Church. Today, a variety of unconventional and more colorful dried fruits and nuts are used in place of the four original toppings. My favorite part of making *mendiants* is the artful process of arranging the colorful bits on a blank canvas of melted chocolate.

Although these candies are easy to assemble, the chocolate requires tempering, which can be tricky. The method I recommend and use is called seeding. It doesn't require special tempering equipment, and anyone can do it with standard tools from their own kitchen.

1½ pounds finely chopped dark chocolate (not chocolate chips)

Assortment of dried fruits and nuts: pistachios, cranberries, candied orange peel, and almonds

---

1. To temper the chocolate, lay several sheets of parchment paper on a work surface or line several baking sheets with parchment paper.

2. Place two-thirds of the chocolate in a metal bowl and place the bowl over a saucepan of simmering water. The water should be gently simmering, not boiling, and the bottom of the metal bowl should not touch the water. Avoid getting water into the chocolate as you melt it over the simmering water. One accidental drop and the chocolate will seize—that is, turn grainy and harden in a chunky mass.

3. Insert a candy or chocolate thermometer into the chocolate. Carefully fold the chocolate with a rubber spatula to ensure even heating as it melts.

4. Bring the chocolate to 120°F. Do not let it exceed this temperature, or the chocolate will bloom. When chocolate blooms, the butterfat rises to the surface as the chocolate solidifies, creating an unsightly white coating.

5. Remove the metal bowl from the simmering water and wipe the condensation from the bottom of the bowl with a dishtowel.

6. Add the remaining chocolate a little at a time. Stir, waiting until each addition is melted before adding the next. Continue adding the chocolate, stirring until smooth.

7. When the chocolate's temperature drops to 82°F, return the metal bowl to the simmering water and bring the temperature to 88°F. Do not allow it to go higher, or you will need to reheat

it again to 120°F and reseed the melted mass with more chopped chocolate.

8. Quickly spoon small dollops of chocolate onto the prepared parchment and gently spread them into rough circles.

9. Top the chocolate with your choice of dried fruits and nuts.

10. Allow the candies to harden. Peel from the parchment and transfer to a tin.

OTHER TOPPING IDEAS

- Candied citron
- Cashews
- Dragées
- Dried mango
- Glacé cherries
- Hazelnuts
- Nonpareils
- Pine nuts
- Pretzels
- Sea salt

PINK PEPPERCORN
MACARONS

YIELD: Approximately 18 sandwich cookies

Pink peppercorns have a beautiful pink-red skin and are often used as a colorful garnish. The inner kernel's slightly hot and fruity bite goes well with sweet and savory dishes alike.

I couldn't resist pairing delicate *macaron* shells with the equally delicate pink peppercorn. Note: The skins are easily removed from peppercorns by rubbing them between your fingers.

MACARONS
- ¾ cup almond flour
- 1 cup confectioners' sugar
- 2 egg whites, at room temperature
- Pinch of cream of tartar
- ¼ cup superfine sugar
- ⅛ to ¼ teaspoon pink gel food coloring, such as Americolor Deep Pink or Wilton's Rose
- Skins of 2 tablespoons pink peppercorns
- 15 to 20 whole pink peppercorns

FILLING
- 8 ounces cream cheese, softened
- ¼ pound (1 stick) butter, softened
- 2 cups confectioners' sugar
- 3 to 5 pink peppercorns

Make the *macarons*:

1. Line 2 cookie sheets with parchment paper. Fit a pastry bag with a plain Wilton size 2A tip and set aside.

2. Combine the almond flour and confectioners' sugar in the bowl of a food processor. Pulse a few times in short bursts to combine.

3. In a spotlessly clean bowl, beat the egg whites until foamy.

4. Add the cream of tartar and beat again until soft peaks form. Reduce the mixer speed to low and gradually add the superfine sugar.

5. Increase the speed to high and beat until stiff peaks form.

6. Sift the almond flour over the egg whites and fold until just incorporated. The mixture will be thick.

7. Add the pink food coloring and mix until the dough is shiny and loosened. When the mixture is ready it will fall from the spatula in a thick ribbon.

8. Transfer the dough to the pastry bag with a large rubber spatula.

9. Pipe 1½-inch rounds on the prepared cookie sheets.

10. Tap the bottom of the sheet to release any air pockets in the *macarons*.

11. Sprinkle the *macarons* with the pink peppercorn skins. Top half of the *macarons* with a single pink peppercorn.

12. Preheat the oven to 375°F. Let the *macarons* set for 15 to 20 minutes at room temperature.

13. Put 1 sheet of *macarons* in the oven and immediately reduce the oven temperature to

325°F. Bake for 10 minutes, turning the pan halfway through. Remove from the oven.

14. Increase the heat to 375°F and wait 5 minutes. Put the second pan of *macarons* in the oven and, again, decrease the heat to 325°F. Bake 10 minutes, rotating the pan halfway through as before. Let the *macarons* cool on the baking sheets for a few minutes before peeling them off the parchment paper.

Make the filling:
1. Combine the cream cheese and butter in a bowl and beat with a hand mixer on high speed until well incorporated.

2. Decrease the mixer speed to low and beat in the confectioners' sugar.

3. Crush pink peppercorns with the side of a chef's knife and add to the cream cheese mixture.

4. Mix on low speed until the flakes are dispersed. Increase the amount of crushed peppercorns to taste.

5. Spoon or pipe the cream cheese filling onto the center of the plain *macarons* shells and top with the shells that have been embellished with the peppercorns.

POMEGRANATE
PANNA COTTA

YIELD: 6 (¾-cup) servings

This dessert is another example of how beautiful naturally occurring food hues can be. The first time I had this dessert, I was intrigued by the unusual mauve color and the intense tartness the pomegranate juice lends to creamy *panna cotta*.

2½ cups plus 3 tablespoons pure pomegranate juice
2 teaspoons unflavored powdered gelatin
1 cup sugar
2 cups heavy cream
Pomegranate arils (seeds) for garnish

1. Place 3 tablespoons of the pomegranate juice in small bowl and sprinkle the gelatin over it. Let stand until absorbed.

2. Heat 2 cups of the pomegranate juice and the sugar in a saucepan over high heat, stirring constantly to dissolve the sugar.

3. Boil until the juice is reduced to 1¼ cups and the mixture is syrupy, about 10 minutes.

4. Remove from the heat. Transfer ⅓ cup syrup to a small bowl and reserve for the sauce. Allow sauce to come to room temperature, cover bowl in plastic wrap or transfer to an airtight container, and place in the refrigerator to chill for later use.

5. Add the gelatin mixture to the remaining syrup in the saucepan. Stir until the gelatin has completely melted.

6. Add the remaining ½ cup pomegranate juice and the heavy cream; stir well.

7. Strain the mixture through a fine sieve. Divide evenly among dessert cups and refrigerate until set, several hours or overnight.

8. Drizzle the sauce over the top and garnish with pomegranate seeds before serving.

Note: If inverting the *panna cotta* from molds or ramekins, spray with cooking spray before pouring in the liquid. When chilled, run a knife around the edge of the mold before turning the *panna cotta* out.

VANILLA BEAN BABY DOUGHNUTS

YIELD: 60 to 72 baby doughnuts

Doughnuts have never been so cute! Ordinary liquid blue food coloring is mixed with dark vanilla extract in the doughnut glaze to create a pretty robin's-egg blue.

Note: This recipe requires the purchase of a mini-doughnut pan, which can be found inexpensively online or in specialty kitchen stores.

DOUGHNUT BATTER
- 2 cups all-purpose flour, sifted
- ¾ cup sugar
- 2 teaspoons baking powder
- ½ teaspoon salt
- ¾ cup buttermilk
- 2 eggs, lightly beaten
- 1 teaspoon pure vanilla extract
- Seeds from one vanilla bean
- 2 tablespoons butter, melted

VANILLA GLAZE
- 1 cup confectioners' sugar
- 1 tablespoon milk
- ½ teaspoon vanilla extract
- 4 drops of liquid blue food coloring
- White nonpareils

Make the doughnut batter:

1. Preheat the oven to 425°F.

2. In large mixing bowl, sift together the flour, sugar, baking powder, and salt. Add the buttermilk, eggs, vanilla extract, vanilla seeds, and butter and beat until just combined.

3. Spray the doughnut cavities with cooking spray or brush them with butter.

4. Transfer the batter to a piping bag without a tip or a zip-top bag with the corner snipped off. Fill each doughnut cup approximately halfway.

5. Bake 5 to 8 minutes or until the top of the doughnuts spring back when touched. Let cool in the pan for 4 to 5 minutes before removing.

Make the vanilla glaze:

1. In a small bowl, stir together the sugar, milk, and vanilla extract until the sugar is completely dissolved.

2. Add the food coloring and stir until the color is uniform.

3. Immediately dip the doughnuts into the glaze. Let stand briefly for the glaze to set.

4. Sprinkle on the nonpareils.

Note: Doughnuts are best when eaten the same day they are baked.

you can also use a zip-top bag with the corner snipped

A. Put the doughnut batter in a piping bag so you can easily fill the doughnut molds. **B.** Fill the doughnut cavities. **C.** Once the doughnuts are baked, they are ready to be glazed. **D.** Decorate the glazed doughnuts with white nonpareils.

YEMA CANDY

YIELD: Approximately 17 candies

This dessert first originated in Spain, and is now largely regarded as a Filipino dish. In my research I've found a number of recipes for *yema* candy—each different in some small way. Some have nuts, some have a hard caramel coating, and some contain milk powder. The recipe below is the easiest I've found. It is delicately soft and indulgently sweet.

1 tablespoon butter
1 (14-ounce) can sweetened condensed milk
5 egg yolks
½ cup of pistachios, very finely chopped (optional)
Yellow sanding sugar

1. Melt the butter in a medium saucepan over medium heat.

2. Add the sweetened condensed milk and stir. Heat for 1 minute. Add the egg yolks and stir again.

3. When the egg yolks are incorporated, add the pistachios, if desired.

4. Keep stirring until the *yema* forms a thick paste and pulls away from the sides of the saucepan. Remove from the heat and transfer to a bowl. Let cool completely.

5. Once the candy has cooled, shape into 1½-inch balls and roll in the sanding sugar. If the mixture is sticky, butter your hands before you roll each candy into a ball.

Yema candy is traditionally wrapped individually in colorful cellophane papers. *Yema* means "yolk" in Spanish.

MIXED MEDIA

An artist using any combination of media—
acrylic paint, colored pencils, plaster, etc.—on a
single canvas is creating mixed media artwork.
Aimed at taking your baking artistry up a notch,
the recipes in this section draw upon the skills
you've gained in the rest of this book. These
are not "everyday" desserts—patience and
persistence are required!

MIXED MEDIA

THINGS TO KEEP IN MIND

▇ Implement several art forms into one project. A gingerbread house is a perfect example of mixed media baking. An artist's brush and food coloring can be used to paint on fine details. The gingerbread house itself is a sculpture and is made using various forms of media: gingerbread, royal icing, candies, and nonpareils.

▇ Look for inspiration everywhere. Find three-dimensional objects that you love, and think about ways to re-create them in your baking. Find color palettes that inspire you, even if it's from the paint-chip section at the hardware store. Study textiles, newsprint, paintings, logos . . . anything you can pull a feature from to easily re-create as a confection. Think about how you can bring all of these elements together into one piece of confectionery art.

▇ After you've found inspiration, plan the design. Don't be afraid to do a rough sketch on paper. This can often give you an idea of the size and shape the artwork should be and what materials you will require to complete the idea.

▇ Make a list of all the art materials you will need ahead of time. Ask yourself: "What should I make first? Do I need paintbrushes? What size? How much fondant will I need? How much cake will I need? What embellishments require extra drying time?" Try to tackle the specifics before you preheat the oven. Getting organized ahead of time will make assembling the work far more enjoyable.

▇ Be playful! Mixed media projects take a lot of time, which is reason enough to keep them fun and lighthearted. Don't be discouraged if something doesn't turn out exactly as planned. Cake is fragile. Fondant will sometimes tear. Accidents happen. Just remember to have fun and not take it too seriously. The more you enjoy the endeavor, the more you'll want to challenge your baking talents.

SOUTHERN BOMBE

YIELD: 12 to 15 servings

This combines all my southern favorites in a stunning ice-cream cake. A red velvet roulade with cream cheese center surrounds buttermilk ice cream and whipped chocolate ganache.

RED VELVET CAKE
4 eggs
¾ cup superfine sugar
1 tablespoon vegetable oil
2 tablespoons buttermilk
1 teaspoon vinegar
1 teaspoon vanilla extract
1 ounce (2 tablespoons) red food coloring
¾ cup cake flour, sifted
¼ cup cocoa powder
1 teaspoon baking powder
½ teaspoon salt
Confectioners' sugar, for rolling the cake

CREAM CHEESE FILLING
8 ounces cream cheese, softened
1 cup confectioners' sugar

4 tablespoons butter, softened
1 teaspoon vanilla extract

ICE CREAM
6 egg yolks
¾ cup sugar
1 cup heavy cream
2 cups buttermilk

SWEETENED WHIPPED CREAM
1½ cups heavy cream
¾ cup superfine sugar

CHOCOLATE GANACHE
9 ounces semisweet or bittersweet chocolate
1 cup heavy cream

Make the red velvet cake:

1. Preheat the oven to 350°F. Grease a jelly roll pan with shortening. Line the pan with parchment paper and grease the paper also.

2. Place the eggs in a stand mixer fitted with the whisk attachment, and with a timer set, beat for 5 minutes.

3. Slowly add the sugar and oil. Beat well. Add the buttermilk, vinegar, vanilla, and red food coloring. Switch to the paddle attachment.

4. Sift together the flour, cocoa powder, baking powder, and salt, and slowly add to the liquid ingredients. Beat for 2 minutes, until well combined. The batter will be very thin.

5. Pour the batter into the prepared jelly roll pan and bake for 12 to 15 minutes. When done, the cake should spring back when touched in the center.

6. As the cake bakes, sprinkle a thin tea towel with a generous amount of confectioners' sugar.

7. When the cake is done, immediately turn it out onto the towel and remove the parchment paper. Starting from the narrow end, roll the cake into the tea towel. Place the cake seam-side down on a cooling rack for 30 minutes.

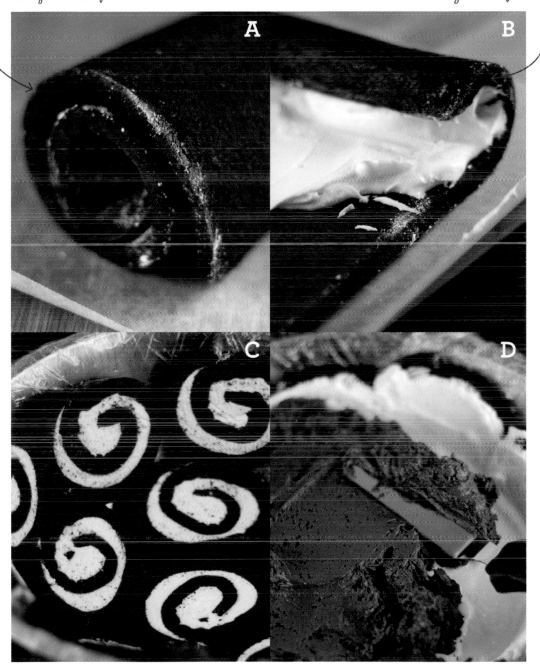

the cake holds its curl
after being rolled up

let the end of the cake curl
while you are frosting it

A. The red velvet cake will look like this after being rolled and cooled. B. Fill the cake with cream cheese frosting. C. Line a 4-quart bowl with pieces of roulade. D. Spread whipped chocolate ganache over the buttermilk ice cream.

Make the cream cheese filling:

1. Combine the cream cheese, confectioners' sugar, butter, and vanilla, and beat well with an electric hand mixer.

2. Gently unroll the cake, remove the tea towel, and transfer the cake to a sheet of wax paper. Spread the filling evenly over the surface.

3. Reroll the cake, thereby creating the roulade.

4. Wrap the roulade in the wax paper and some plastic wrap and refrigerate until ready to use.

Make the ice cream:

1. Whisk the egg yolks and sugar together in a medium bowl until thick and pale yellow.

2. Heat the heavy cream in a medium saucepan over medium-high heat until just boiling.

3. Slowly pour the cream into the egg mixture, whisking constantly.

4. Return the mixture to the saucepan and heat over medium-low heat, stirring with a wooden spoon, until the mixture is has thickened and coats the back of the spoon.

5. Pour the mixture into a clean bowl and stir in the buttermilk.

6. Cover and refrigerate until chilled, about 1 hour.

7. Freeze in an ice cream maker according to the manufacturer's directions

Make the sweetened whipped cream:

1. In a large bowl, whip the heavy cream on high speed until soft peaks are formed.

2. Add the superfine sugar slowly, 1 to 2 tablespoons at a time, until it has dissolved and the cream forms stiff peaks.

3. Cover and place in the refrigerator until ready to use.

Make the chocolate ganache:

1. Roughly chop the chocolate and place in a medium bowl.

2. In a small saucepan, heat the heavy cream over medium-high heat until just boiling.

3. Pour the hot cream over the chocolate and whisk until the chocolate is melted and the mixture is smooth.

4. Allow to cool slightly.

5. Pour the cooled ganache into the bowl of a mixer and beat on high with the whisk attachment for 5 minutes.

Note: The ganache can be made after the cake is completely assembled and frozen.

Assemble the bombe:

1. Remove the roulade from the refrigerator and unwrap. Cut the roulade evenly into ¾-inch-thick round slices.

2. Line a 4-quart stainless steel mixing bowl with several long sheets of plastic wrap, and allow the edges to hang over the sides of the bowl. Line the bowl with the roulade pieces, placing them as closely together as possible.

3. Completely cover the roulade pieces with the sweetened whipped cream, spreading thickly to make sure the spaces between the rounds are covered.

4. Freeze the cake and whipped cream layer for 30 minutes.

5. Remove the ice cream from the freezer and let stand until softened enough to stir.

6. Remove the cake from the freezer and pour the buttermilk ice cream over the cake and whipped cream layer. Use a spatula to smooth out the top.

7. Cover with plastic wrap, place the bowl in the freezer, and allow the ice cream layer to harden, approximately 2 to 4 hours. Top with whipped chocolate ganache. Freeze for an additional 30 minutes.

8. Turn the entire cake out onto a plate or cake stand. The cake can be finished by piping rosettes of whipped cream between the roulade slices and around the base of the serving plate. Cut into slices and serve with additional sweetened whipped cream, if desired.

GLITTERING COOKIE TREE

YIELD: 75 cookies and 1 tree

This colorful and eye-catching centerpiece involves equal parts baking and crafting. The cookies are gently pressed into a pressed-foam cone coated with buttercream, which means it's not just pretty but delicious as well! Guests will feel like they are in a real-life Candyland as they pluck sugared bites from the cookie tree.

SUGAR COOKIES
- 1⅓ cups all-purpose flour
- ⅔ cup cornstarch
- ¼ teaspoon salt
- ½ pound (2 sticks) butter, softened
- ½ cup confectioners' sugar
- 1 teaspoon vanilla
- Colored sanding sugars

BUTTERCREAM
- ¼ pound (1 stick) butter, softened
- 1½ to 2 cups confectioners' sugar
- 1 teaspoon vanilla extract
- Milk or heavy cream, optional

EQUIPMENT
- 1 (10-inch) pressed-foam cone

Make the sugar cookies:

1. Preheat the oven to 350°F. Line 2 large baking sheets with parchment paper.

2. Whisk together the flour, cornstarch, and salt.

3. Beat together the butter and confectioners' sugar with an electric mixer until pale and fluffy. Beat in the vanilla.

4. At low speed, mix the flour mixture into the butter mixture just until a soft dough forms.

5. Roll the dough into teaspoon-size balls and place on a baking sheet. Put each color sanding sugar in its own small bowl. Drop the balls into the sanding sugar, turning to coat. Reshape if necessary and return to the baking sheet,

spacing the balls ¾ inch apart. Chill sugar-coated dough balls in the refrigerator for 10 minutes.

6. Bake until the tops are slightly cracked but still pale (the bottoms will be pale golden), 12 to 15 minutes. Transfer the cookies to a rack to cool completely.

Make the buttercream:

1. In a stand mixer fitted with the whisk attachment, mix together the butter and confectioners' sugar on low speed until crumbly. Increase to high speed and beat for 3 minutes.

2. Add the vanilla extract and beat again for another minute. If you find that the buttercream is too stiff, you may add milk or heavy cream, 1 tablespoon at a time, until the mixture reaches spreading consistency.

Assemble the cookie tree:

1. Choose a serving platter: a plate, cake stand, or cake board will work well. Cover the bottom of the cone with icing and press the cone into the plate. This will hold it steadfast as you coat the outside with icing.

2. Cover the cone with a ½-inch-thick layer of buttercream on all sides and across the top.

3. Layer the cookies onto the cone, gently pressing them into the buttercream. The tree is best assembled the day of your party, though it can stand for 2 days at room temperature.

D

the icing is the adhesive

A. Roll the dough balls in sparkling sanding sugar. B. Bake the cookies. C. Use a Styrofoam cone as the foundation of the cookie tree. D. Layer the cookies on the buttercream-frosted Styrofoam cone.

YULE LOG CAKE

YIELD: Serves 8

This is my tongue-in-cheek take on the classic Yule log cake, based on the shape of a Duraflame® log. *Génoise* cake is stacked—not rolled—between layers of decadent chocolate ganache. The rolled fondant exterior is hand-faux-finished as realistic wood grain. This project implements all three elements discussed in this book: line, sculpture, and color.

CHOCOLATE GANACHE FILLING
- 1 cup semisweet chocolate chips
- 1 cup heavy cream
- 2 tablespoons butter

GÉNOISE
- 2 eggs
- ¼ cup superfine sugar
- ½ cup all-purpose flour
- 1 teaspoon orange extract
- 2 teaspoons orange zest
- Confectioners' sugar, for dusting

ASSEMBLY
- ½ cup orange marmalade, melted
- Confectioners' sugar, for rolling
- 1 cup marzipan (see page 78)
- Orange gel food coloring
- Brown gel food coloring
- 1 cup white fondant (see page 74)
- ¼ cup *crème de cacao*
- ¼ cup Graham cracker crumbs

EQUIPMENT
- Small round artist's brush, such as round number 3
- Artist's natural sea sponge
- Pastry comb

Make the chocolate ganache filling:

1. Pour the chocolate chips into a medium bowl.

2. In a saucepan, heat the heavy cream over medium heat until very hot, but not boiling.

3. Pour the hot cream over the chocolate chips and let stand for 2 minutes.

4. Whisk together the cream and chocolate until smooth.

5. Add the butter and stir until melted.

6. Refrigerate until the mixture is of spreading consistency, about 1 hour.

Make the *génoise*:

1. Preheat the oven to 350°F. Grease and line a 9 x 13-inch jelly roll pan with parchment paper; grease the paper. Fill a saucepan halfway with water and bring to a simmer over medium heat.

2. Using an electric hand mixer, beat together the eggs and sugar in a heatproof bowl.

3. Place the bowl over the simmering water and continue to beat with the hand mixer until thick and pale.

4. Remove the bowl from the heat and continue beating until the mixture is cool and leaves a thick trail of batter when the beaters are lifted from the bowl.

5. Sift the flour onto the surface and add the orange extract and zest.

6. Carefully fold the flour, extract, and zest into the whipped eggs and sugar with a rubber spatula. Pour into the prepared jelly roll pan.

7. Tilt the pan or use an offset spatula to level the batter, and bake for approximately 10 minutes, or until the cake springs back when touched lightly with a fingertip.

8. Spread a thin tea towel on a work surface and sprinkle generously with confectioners' sugar. When the cake is done, invert onto the sugared tea towel, remove the parchment, and trim the edges of the cake. The trimmed cake should measure approximately 8 x 12 inches.

Assemble the cake:

1. Cut the cake into 4 (4 x 8-inch) pieces.

2. Frost three cake layers with the ganache, stack them, and top with the fourth layer. If any of the layers are uneven, trim to square off the sides. Frost the sides and ends of the cake. Leave the top of the cake unfrosted.

3. Brush the top of the cake with the marmalade. Dust a work surface with confectioners' sugar and roll the marzipan to ¼ inch thick.

4. Measure the top, sides, and end of the cake, and cut the marzipan pieces to size. Press the marzipan pieces into the cake sides, edges, and top.

5. Knead both gel food colorings into the fondant a little at a time until a muted tan-orange color is achieved.

6. Add up the measurements of the length and height of the cake to find the total circumference and width. Sprinkle a work surface with confectioners' sugar and roll the fondant large enough to completely cover the top and long sides of the cake, using your measurements as a guide.

7. With two large spatulas, lift the cake and set it on the narrow fondant end closest to you. With an X-Acto knife, trim the fondant flush with the bottom edge of the cake.

8. Brush the top and sides of the marzipan-covered cake with marmalade. Lift the top edge of the fondant up and over the cake (toward you) and drape it as if wrapping a box with paper. Use your hands to smooth the fondant, removing any air bubbles and adhering it to the marzipan. The top end of the fondant should now meet the trimmed edge at the bottom of the front of the cake. Use an X-Acto knife to cut the excess fondant at the seam, cutting it flush with the other fondant edge. Trim the sides of the fondant flush with the ends of the cake.

9. Reroll the remaining fondant scraps and measure two squares to fit over the two ends of the cake. Brush the ends with marmalade and press the fondant squares onto the cake.

10. Measure 1 teaspoon of brown food coloring and pour in a small condiment cup. Dilute with a few drops of *crème de cacao*.

11. To apply the faux finish to the cake, beginning at the end of the cake and using a small round artist's brush, paint two circles in the bottom left-hand corner to create tree rings. Continue to paint circles radiating outward from the two circles, in varying thickness. This pattern doesn't have to be perfect; in fact, it is better if it is asymmetrical and rustic-looking.

12. Continue drawing half circles outward, redipping the paintbrush as needed. When the end of the cake is covered, repeat the process on the other end of the cake.

13. Dip the paintbrush in the brown food coloring and blot the bristles on a paper towel until almost dry. Dry-brush the ends of the cake, using strokes that radiate out from the center "tree ring."

A. Layer chocolate ganache between the cake pieces. **B.** Apply the orange marmalade to the cake with a pastry brush. **C.** Cover the cake on all sides with marzipan. **D.** Lay a tinted piece of fondant over the marmalade-brushed marzipan as the final layer.

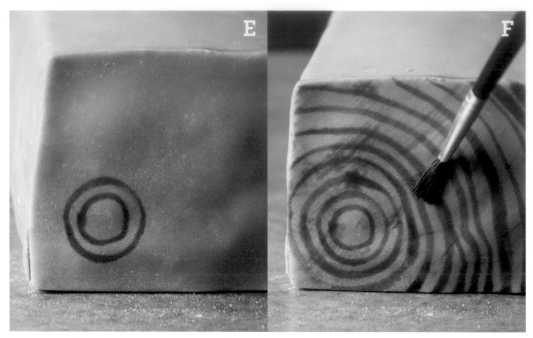

E. Paint circles, starting in the lower left-hand corner, to create the "tree rings" in the wood. **F.** Use a dry brush to create striations in the faux wood finish.

14. In a separate condiment cup, pour a small amount of undiluted brown gel food coloring. Load the paintbrush and make a dark dot in the middle of the "tree ring." Retrace a few lines previously made by the diluted paint with a well-loaded brush of undiluted paint.

15. When finished retracing the lines, use the tip of the artist's brush to create fine cracks radiating from the center "tree ring" and randomly outward to the right. Be sure to repeat this process on the other end of the cake.

16. Using the diluted paint, make several graduated V-shaped marks, beginning with a small V in the center-top of the cake and graduating downward to large V shapes. Retrace a few of the Vs with undiluted paint, as you did with the end piece.

17. Create a "wood stain" by diluting the remaining undiluted brown gel food coloring with *crème de cacao*. If you have a spare piece of rolled fondant, test the stain for lightness by dipping the artist's sponge in the diluted mixture, then rubbing it on with one or two swipes. The stain should be light brown and transparent.

18. Rub the stain over the hand-painting and on all sides of the cake.

19. Drag the pastry comb through the stain on either side of the cake and over the top of the cake in two undulating strokes.

Note: A rubber wood-grain comb can be purchased at most home improvement stores.

20. To finish the cake, moisten the graham cracker crumbs with leftover *crème de cacao*–food coloring stain. Place the cake on a long serving dish and surround with the crumbs.

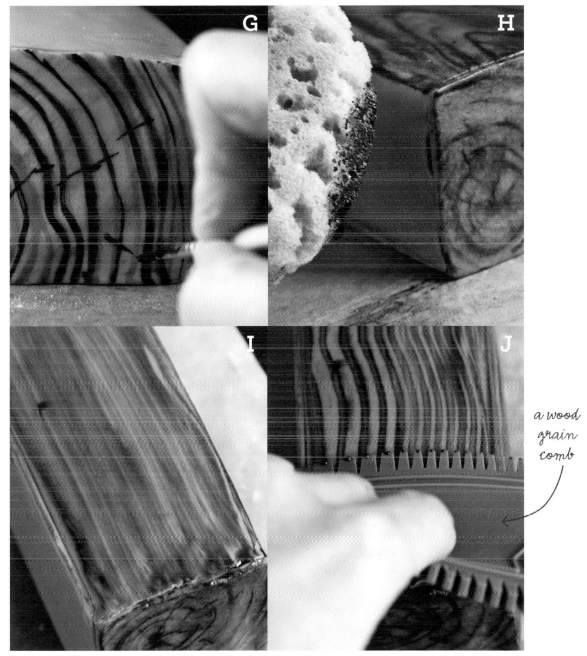

a wood grain comb

G. Use undiluted brown food coloring to make darker wood grain. **H.** Use a sponge to apply the "varnish" made from *crème de cacao* and brown food coloring. **I.** A "varnished" side of the cake. **J.** Use a pastry comb or wood grain tool to make even striations on the fondant surface.

ANATOMICAL HEART CAKE

YIELD: 8 to 10 servings

Use this sculptural Black Forest cake as a symbol of your undying love for Valentine's Day—or if your true love is squeamish, surprise guests at your next zombie movie night.

CAKE
½ pound (2 sticks) butter, softened
1½ cups packed light brown sugar
2 eggs, at room temperature
6 tablespoons unsweetened cocoa powder
1½ teaspoons baking soda
1 teaspoon vanilla extract
¼ teaspoon salt
1½ cups all-purpose flour, sifted
⅔ cup sour cream, at room temperature
¾ cup hot coffee

FROSTING
½ pound (2 sticks) butter, softened
4 cups confectioners' sugar
4 tablespoons unsweetened cocoa powder, sifted

GRISLY BITS
2 (15-ounce) cans pitted dark sweet cherries, well drained
1 pound fondant tinted red (see page 74)
Blue gel food coloring
Confectioners' sugar
Corn syrup or piping gel

CHERRY GLAZE PLASMA
¼ teaspoon red gel food coloring
2 tablespoons corn syrup

Make the cake:

1. Preheat the oven to 350°F. Grease a 9-inch round cake pan and line the bottom with parchment. Grease the parchment.

2. Using an electric mixer, beat the butter in a large bowl until smooth.

3. Add the sugar and eggs; beat until lightened in color.

4. Add the cocoa, baking soda, vanilla extract, and salt; mix well.

5. Beat in the flour in 3 additions alternately with the sour cream, beginning and ending with the flour.

6. Add the hot coffee and mix until a smooth, thin batter forms.

7. Pour the batter into the prepared pan. Bake until a toothpick tester comes out clean, approximately 40 minutes.

8. Cool the cake in the pan for 10 minutes before inverting and cooling completely on a rack. Store the cake in an airtight container until ready for use.

Make the frosting:

1. In the bowl of a stand mixer fitted with the whisk attachment, cream together the butter,

A. Make a rough carving of the cake. B. Split the cake and fill it with frosting and black cherries. C. Replace the top and frost the entire cake. D. Cover the cake with red fondant with blue and red marbling. E. Use your fingers to sculpt the top of the cake. F. Fold in the top of the fondant "artery" for a finished look.

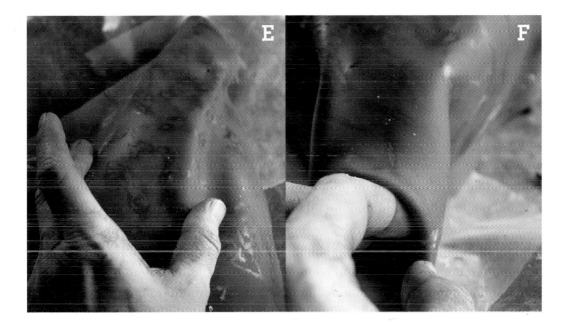

sugar, and cocoa, beginning on low speed then increasing the speed to high.

2. Beat until fluffy and lightened in color.

Assemble the cake:

1. Using a large serrated knife, trim the cake into a triangular shape with rounded corners.

2. Trim two of the edges from the top edge of the corner downward, creating a roughly sculpted three-dimensional anatomical heart shape. Split the cake horizontally into two layers.

3. Spread about ¾ cup buttercream on the bottom layer and arrange about 15 cherries on the frosted layer. Reserve the remaining cherries for the cherry glaze "plasma."

4. Line a serving platter with wax paper strips. Replace the top layer of the cake, transfer the cake to the serving platter, and frost with buttercream. Let stand until the buttercream crusts.

5. To cover the cake, add a small amount of blue gel food coloring to the red fondant

and knead, folding two or three times. Do not over-mix.

6. Measure the cake. Dust a stainproof work surface with confectioners' sugar and roll the fondant with a large fondant rolling pin. Roll the fondant to ¼-inch thickness. Fondant should be about twice the size of the cake measurements. Lay the fondant over the cake. Position the fondant so there is a large over-hang of fondant at the top of the cake, but still plenty of fondant at the bottom of the cake.

7. Cut away excess fondant around the "bulb" of the heart (everything except the "artery" at the top of the cake), leaving a 2-inch margin to tuck under the cake. Reserve excess fondant for later use.

8. Tuck excess fondant under the cake by gently lifting the cake with an offset spatula and folding the fondant under the cake. The weight of the cake will help seal the fondant edges. Use the uncut fondant at the top of the cake to create a tubelike shape, or "artery."

G. Reserve a small piece of fondant. **H.** Roll the reserved piece of fondant into an artery.

9. Use corn syrup or piping gel to seal the artery ends together. Fold a portion of the tube inward to create a clean edge.

10. Sculpt the heart's artery further by pressing your fingers into the icing on either side of the fondant tube and pulling your fingers downward to create an impression.

11. Cut a rolled piece of fondant into a 4 x 4-inch square and fold the top ½ inch inward.

12. Brush corn syrup on one short edge of the piece and roll the fondant into a tube, pressing the cut edges together to seal. Using your fingers, flare the bottom portion slightly by pinching the edges and pulling them outward slightly.

13. Brush the flared edge with corn syrup and place to the left of the large artery. Press a toothpick into the cake inside the tube to anchor the artery to the main cake until it dries.

14. Cut another piece of rolled fondant to 6 x 10 inches. This does not have to be perfectly square; just use whatever fondant scraps are left to approximate the size. Fold 1 inch of fondant inward and roll the fondant piece lengthwise into a tube, leaving the bottom portion open. You are making an artery with a large flat end. This piece will be placed to the right of the large artery. Apply corn syrup to the edges and press to adhere into the cake.

Make the cherry glaze "plasma":
1. Puree ½ cup of the remaining dark sweet cherries (left over from the cake assembly) in a food processor or blender.

2. Combine the cherry puree, food coloring, and corn syrup in a small saucepan and gently cook until combined. Let cool.

3. Glaze the entire cake with the cherry sauce. Serve the cake with the remaining cherries on the side.

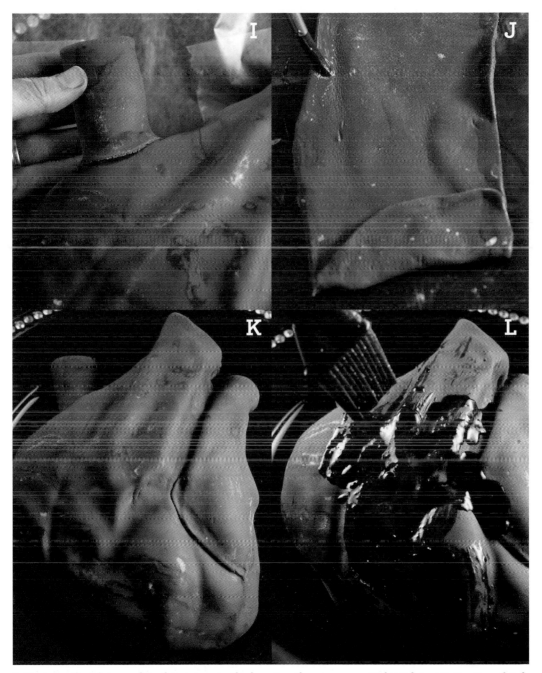

I. Use a toothpick to anchor this artery to the heart as the corn syrup "glue" dries. J. Create a third artery is using a long piece of fondant. K. Finished fondant work. L. Cover the cake in a cherry glaze "plasma."

BREAKFAST FOR DESSERT

YIELD: 8 to 10 custard eggs and lollipops

My play on boiled eggs and toast soldiers is a sweet combo of boiled vanilla custard and mango puree poured into sterilized eggshells. Like the original savory toast version, the shortbread soldiers are used for dipping into the faux yolk.

Morning coffee has been made extra sweet in the form of a lollipop. It can be enjoyed as is or you can serve it in a brewed cup to stir in strength and sweetness.

EGGSHELLS
  8 jumbo eggs or 10 large eggs

CUSTARD
  1 cup milk (or use heavy cream for
    richer custard)
  ¼ cup sugar
  2 eggs, lightly beaten
  ¼ teaspoon vanilla extract

MANGO "YOLK"
  1 medium ripe mango
  2 tablespoons sugar
  ¼ teaspoon lemon juice

SHORTBREAD
  ½ pound (2 sticks) butter, softened
  2 tablespoons granulated sugar
  ½ cup confectioners' sugar

  1 teaspoon vanilla extract
  2 cups all-purpose flour, plus more for
    rolling
  ¼ teaspoon salt

COFFEE LOLLIPOPS
  White vegetable shortening for
    greasing the pan
  1 cup sugar
  ⅓ cup freshly brewed espresso or very
    darkly brewed coffee—the stronger
    the coffee, the better!
  1 tablespoon light corn syrup
  ¼ teaspoon unsweetened cocoa
    powder (not Dutch process)
  ¼ teaspoon ground cinnamon
  ½ teaspoon pure vanilla extract
  8 to 10 lollipop sticks

Prepare the eggshells:

1. Preheat the oven to 200°F. Place a cooling rack over a baking tray.

2. Crack the eggs by tapping them with a spoon on the most pointed end. Once the egg tip is cracked, pinch away just enough of the eggshell top for the egg white and yolk to pour out.

3. Reserve 2 whole eggs for the custard and save the rest for another use. Wash the shells

in warm water. Rub your finger on the inside to remove any bits of the membrane.

4. Place the cleaned eggshells upside-down on the cooling rack and bake for 20 to 25 minutes. Let the sterilized eggshells cool completely before you fill them with the custard.

Note: Stand the eggshells upright in a carton to fill.

Make the custard:

1. In a small saucepan, whisk together the milk and sugar and place over medium heat.

2. Heat until the milk is very hot but not boiling. Remove from the heat.

3. Whisk constantly while you gradually pour the eggs into the milk, taking care to temper the mixture slowly (you don't want scrambled eggs in your custard).

4. Return the pan to medium heat and whisk constantly until the mixture has thickened and is just beginning to bubble.

5. Remove from the heat and stir in the vanilla. Transfer the mixture to a pitcher with a spout.

6. Pour the custard evenly into the eggshells, at least three-quarters full, and refrigerate until firm.

Make the mango "yolk":

1. Peel and cut the mango into chunks.

2. Puree the flesh with the sugar and lemon juice in a food processor or blender. Transfer the sweetened puree to a piping bag without a tip or to a zip-top bag with a corner snipped off.

3. When the custards are firm, spoon out a small portion in the middle, creating a well for the mango puree.

4. Pipe in the mango puree and return the custards to the refrigerator until ready for serving.

Make the shortbread:

1. Preheat the oven to 350°F. Cover a baking sheet with parchment paper.

2. In a stand mixer fitted with the paddle attachment, beat the butter and granulated sugar until well combined.

3. Add confectioners' sugar and beat until incorporated. Add vanilla extract and mix again.

4. Add 1 cup of the flour and the salt, and mix on low speed until a dough forms. Add the remaining 1 cup of flour and mix again on low until a very stiff dough forms.

5. Gather the dough together with your hands and place it on a lightly floured surface. Using a floured rolling pin, roll the dough until flattened to about a 1-inch thickness. Wrap the dough in plastic film and place on a cookie sheet or jelly roll pan. Refrigerate for 30 minutes. This dough will firm up quickly because of the high butter content. If your dough is difficult to roll, let it stand at room temperature for a few minutes until it is pliable.

6. While the dough is still cold, on a floured surface, roll it out to a ¼-inch thickness and transfer to the prepared baking sheet. Score with the tines of a fork. You can cut the dough into shapes with a cookie cutter, or bake the entire piece and cut them into "soldiers" after baking, while still hot.

7. Bake the entire dough piece for 20 to 25 minutes or:

- 7 to 10 minutes for small cookies
- 12 to 15 minutes for medium cookies
- 17 to 20 minutes for large cookies

When done, the shortbread will be golden brown around the edges and fragrant.

Make the lollipops:

1. Grease 2 metal baking sheets with the shortening. Stagger the lollipop sticks on the sheets to give the candy plenty of room to spread when you pour the hot mixture.

2. In a medium saucepan, combine the sugar, espresso, corn syrup, cocoa, and cinnamon. Clip a candy thermometer to the side of the saucepan and place over medium heat, stirring until the sugar has dissolved. Simmer until the mixture reaches 290°F.

3. Remove the pan from the heat and stir in the vanilla. The mixture may sputter and bubble a little. Using a metal (or heatproof) 1 tablespoon measure, dip the candy by the heaping tablespoon and pour over the end of the lollipop sticks. Let cool at room temperature until hardened. To remove the lollipops from the baking sheet, gently push the candy with your fingers or a spoon to slide the candy off the edge of the baking sheet. Do not try to lift it or the lollipops may crack.

4. Wrap the lollipops in cellophane candy wrappers or store in an airtight container. They will stay fresh for 1 month.

VARIATION

Mix ½ to 1 teaspoon of espresso powder into the ⅓ cup hot coffee before adding it to the saucepan. I loved this highly caffeinated super-strength treat!

PRESENTATION COUNTS!

Serve the custard eggs in a decorative egg crate, or pile sugar on a plate to hold the eggs upright. Serve with shortbread soldiers for dipping and the coffee lollipops on the side.

BOOK CAKE

YIELD: Serves 12 to 15

I could spend hours engrossed in the intricate artwork of Su Blackwell. Her repurposed book sculptures are hauntingly beautiful, with their fairy-tale and woodland themes. Words take flight in this book cake based on her butterfly book sculpture *The Quiet American*; it's a delicious and visually lovely lesson in line and sculpture techniques.

CAKE

   1 large-batch recipe vanilla
      Madeira cake (see page 42)
   Flavored syrup of your choice,
      optional (see page 35)
   2 cups vanilla American buttercream
      (see page 80)
   1 pound white fondant (see page 74)
   1 pound chocolate fondant (see page 74)
   Confectioner's sugar, for rolling
   Corn syrup
   Black gel food coloring

BUTTERFLY TEMPLATE (see page 265)

EQUIPMENT

   10 x 10 x 2-inch square cake pan
   2 (10 x 14-inch) cake boards

Large serrated knife
Large fondant roller
Ruler
X-Acto knife
Fondant smoother
Serrated quilting wheel for fondant
Artist's brush
Rubber stamps with detail of
   handwritten, calligraphed, or
   typed words
8 sheets of plain wafer paper
Natural bleached white wood stems
   or twigs from the craft store's floral
   department

Make the cake:

1. Bake the large-batch *Madeira* cake in the 10 x 2-inch square cake pan.

2. When the cake is completely cooled, transfer it to a cake board. With a serrated knife, make a vertical slice, without cutting all the way through, halfway into the center of the cake, and carve small pieces away from the slice mark to create the book spine and page crease.

3. Evenly trim the sides of the cake, being careful to retain its square edges, until it measures 9 x 9 inches.

4. After the cake is fully carved, brush it with your choice of flavored simple syrup or leave it plain.

Apply the crumb coat:

1. Ice the cake with a thin, even layer of vanilla American buttercream (crumb coat), maintaining the carved shape; let stand until the buttercream develops a crust.

Note: White buttercream works best under white fondant. A dark buttercream (such as chocolate) will show through the white fondant and make it appear dirty or splotchy.

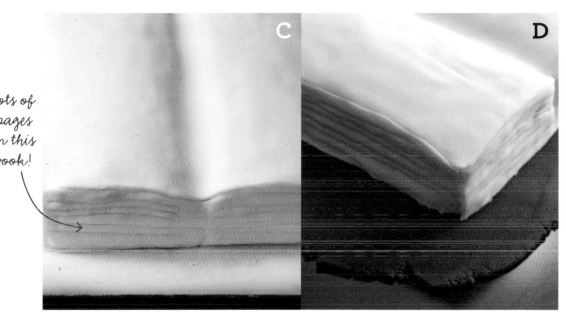

lots of pages in this book!

A. Sturdy _Madeira_ cake makes an excellent, sculpted base (see page 134 for carving tips).
B. Cover the sculpted, frosted cake in fondant. **C.** Score the edges of the cake with the back of a knife to create the illusion of pages. **D.** Use chocolate fondant for the book cover.

Roll the fondant:

1. Dust a large work surface with confectioners' sugar and roll out the white fondant to a ¼-inch thickness with a large fondant rolling pin.

2. Using a ruler, measure the top and sides of the cake and cut individual fondant pieces for each surface. When you are done, you should have 5 pieces; two long pieces for the top and bottom edges of the book, two shorter pieces for the left and right sides of the book, and one large piece for the top surface. The top fondant piece should be slightly larger than the cake to allow for the book crease and rounded pages carved into the cake.

3. Lightly coat the backs of the fondant pieces with a little corn syrup before pressing them into the cake so they're sure to stick. Begin by applying the side and top pieces, and then drape the large surface piece on top.

4. Even up the edges by trimming off excess fondant with the X-Acto knife. Use your fingers to gently press and contour the fondant into the fold you carved earlier. Retrim the edges, if necessary, and use a fondant smoother to iron out any lumps in the fondant. Use the back of a knife or your fingers to tuck the cut edges under the base of the cake.

5. Using the back of a long knife, score long, straight lines around the sides of the cake to mimic stacks of pages. Also make one vertical score in the side of the center of the cake to align with the page crease on each end of the book.

6. Redust the work surface and roll out the chocolate fondant to a ¼-inch thickness. Roll the piece large enough to place the fondant-covered cake in the middle, and have at least a 2-inch excess of fondant on each side.

A butterfly template peeking through wafer paper stamped with food coloring.

7. Transfer the rolled chocolate fondant to the second cake board. Slide the fondant-covered cake off of its board squarely onto the center of the chocolate fondant. Evenly trim a 1½-inch border of chocolate fondant around all four sides of the cake; this creates the book cover. Use your fingers to smooth and round out the edges and create the uneven look of a worn leather book cover.

8. Run the serrated quilting tool around the edge of the book cover to make a seam. If you don't have a quilting tool, you may use a toothpick to make stitch-like impressions around the edge of the chocolate fondant.

Stamp the wafer paper:
1. Thin a small amount of black gel food coloring with a drop or two of water in a small condiment cup. Using the artist's brush, lightly paint the raised portions of the rubber stamp. Be careful not to oversaturate the stamp

because the wafer paper will dissolve under too much moisture.

2. Stamp 4 sheets of wafer paper on the matte side, re-inking as necessary. Space the stamps evenly so the impressions look like paragraphs in a book. Allow the impressions to dry for 5 minutes.

Note: Wafer paper has a matte side and shiny side—avoid stamping the shiny side. The inked rubber stamp tends to stick to the shiny side, which can tear the paper when the stamp is lifted.

3. Cut two of the pieces to fit over the surface of the cake—like two pages of the book. Apply corn syrup to the crease in the center of the cake and press just the inner edges of the two pieces of wafer paper into the corn syrup. Hold it there for a few seconds to make sure it adheres well. Do not adhere the outer edges of the paper; leaving the paper unattached on the outer edges creates a three-dimensional look of paper book pages.

4. Make a butterfly template by tracing the template (see page 265) onto a piece of plain copy paper. On a cutting board, place a piece of stamped wafer paper over the butterfly template and cut around the image with an X-Acto knife. Cut as many butterflies as you can out of the stamped paper.

Note: Make a few butterfly templates in case you accidentally slice through the template.

5. Cut out butterflies from the plain wafer paper in the same manner as the book pages. You can make as many or as few butterflies as you like. You can use extra butterflies to garnish individual pieces of cake.

Make the butterflies in flight:

1. Snap 3 to 5 fine twigs of various lengths from the white stems, and gently press the ends of the stems into the center of the cake (the book fold) so they stand upright.

2. Fold the butterflies in half to simulate flight. Make a tiny hole in the center each of the butterflies and thread them onto the stems. Be careful when doing this: Wafer paper is fragile and will tear.

3. Position the butterflies so they are radiating upward.

PRESENTATION COUNTS!

This cake is presented on a length of cloud wallpaper. It can be found online and in the children's wallpaper section at home stores. To replicate my presentation, cover two pieces of foam-core board or a bifold presentation board with cloud wallpaper. Use the boards as a surface and background for the cake. Use corn syrup to place a few butterflies on the board behind and above the cake for added drama.

TEMPLATES

Most of these templates will require resizing before use, which is a simple task on a modern photocopier or home scanner and printer. Simply increase the size of each image by 25% to 50% increments, until the desired size is achieved.

Marimekko Flower Cookies: Measure about 4 to 6 inches in circumference.

The Queen of Hearts: Face should proportionally fit inside a 4- to 6-inch heart cookie cutter.

Origami Cookies: Crane body and wings should measure about 4 inches from top to bottom.

Tuile Spoons: Should be 6½ inches in length.

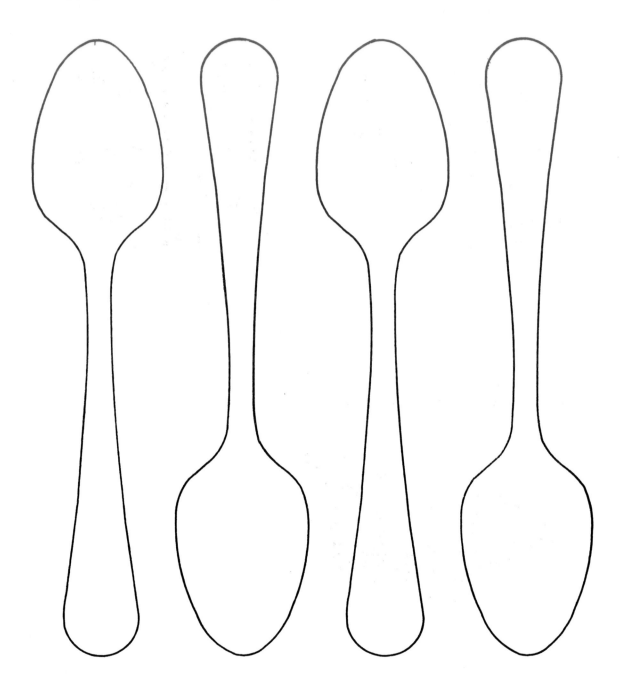

Viking Cake: Rune templates should be used as a guide to draw the banners free-hand.

Book Cake: The wingspan of the butterfly should be approximately four inches across.

HELPFUL BAKING WEBSITES

Not only am I a blogger, but I am an avid blog-reader. Although it is impossible for me to list all the blogs I subscribe to (well over 500), the sites listed here are the ones that I've come to know and love over time. Some are well-known and some are still growing. These blog authors have all inspired me with their recipes, talent, and authenticity. They all feature amazing desserts; some are entirely dedicated to sugary confections, while others feature a mixture of savory and sweet. I hope you'll use these sites as a resource for recipes and inspiration.

Bake at 350—www.bakeat350.blogspot.com

Bake It Pretty blog—http://blog.bakeitpretty. com/

Bakerella—www.bakerella.com

Bakers Royale—www.bakersroyale.com

Baking Banter: The King Arthur Flour Blog— www.kingarthurflour.com/Blog

Bakingdom—www.bakingdom.com

Beatrice Ojakangas— www.beatrice-ojakangas.com; *kransekake* recipe adapted from "The Great Scandinavian Baking Book."

Binnur's Turkish Cookbook— www.turkishcookbook.com; mushroom cookies (MantarKurabiye) adapted from this site.

Bravetart—www.bravetart.com

Cake Central—www.cakecentral.com; piping gel recipe, modeling chocolate and fondant recipe adapted from this site.

Confessions of a Cookbook Queen—www. confessionsofacookbookqueen.com

Cookies and Cups— www.cookiesandcups.blogspot.com

David Leibovitz—www.davidlebovitz.com

Daring Kitchen—www.thedaringkitchen.com; choux puffs recipe, lady fingers recipe and *pâte sablée* recipe adapted from this site.

The Decorated Cookie— www.thedecoratedcookieblog.com

Dessert First—www.dessertfirstgirl.com: seeding method for chocolate adapted from this site.

Domino sugar—www.dominosugar.com; red velvet cake roll recipe used in the southern bombe recipe adapted from this site.

A Dozen Eggs Blog— www.adozeneggs.com/wordpress

Eat the Love—www.eatthelove.com

Epicurious—www.epicurious.com; spice cookie recipe for Mehndi hands; chocolate cake recipe by *Gourmet* magazine; glittering sandwich cookies by *Gourmet* magazine used for glittering cookie tree; *panna cotta* recipe; and pomegranate *panna cotta* recipe all adapted from this site.

Family Fresh Cooking— www.familyfreshcooking.com

Fine Cooking—www.finecooking.com; lemon curd recipe adapted from this site.

Food Network—www.foodnetwork.com; hard candy recipe adapted from Gale Gand.

Heather Ozee Designs—www.heatherozeedesigns.blogspot.com

How Sweet It Is—www.howsweeteats.com

Hungry Rabbit—www.hungryrabbitnyc.com

I Am Baker—www.iammommy.typepad.com/i_am_baker

In the Kitchen and on the Road with Dorie—www.doriegreenspan.com

The Joy of Baking—www.joyofbaking.com; *financiers* recipe adapted from this site.

Lily Vanilli—www.lilyvanilli.com: inspiration for the anatomical heart cake was found at this site.

Martha Stewart Living—www.marthastewart.com; *macaron* recipes adapted from this site.

Matt Bites—www.mattbites.com; candy coating recipe for snow apples recipe adapted from this site.

Munchkin Munchies—www.munchkinmunchies.com

Not Martha—www.notmartha.org

Piece of Cake—www.pieceofcakeblog.blogspot.com

Smitten Kitchen—www.smittenkitchen.com

Sweetapolita—www.sweetapolita.com

Sweetopia—www.sweetopia.net

Tasty Kitchen—www.tastykitchen.com

University of Cookie—www.universityofcookie.com

VerySmall Anna—www.verysmallanna.com

Wilton—www.wilton.com; butter cake recipe and white cake recipe for Neapolitan cake recipe adapted from this site.

USEFUL SUPPLIERS

A.C. MOORE—www.acmoore.com: fondant and fondant tools, decorator tips and piping bags

AMERICOLOR—www.americolorcorp.com: high-quality gel food coloring

ATECO—www.atecousa.com: cake-decorating tools

BAKE IT PRETTY—www.bakeitpretty.com: cupcake papers, cupcake toppers, food colorings, large decorative piping tips, nonpareils

CALLEBAUT—www.callebaut.com: fair-trade-certified high-quality chocolate

FANCY FLOURS—www.fancyflours.com: nonpareils, chocolate transfer paper

GREEN AND BLACK'S CHOCOLATE—www.greenandblacks.com: high-quality organic chocolate; available at many specialty grocery stores such as Whole Foods and Earth Fare; also found at Target

HODGSON MILL—www.hodgsonmill.com: specialty flours such as almond and rice flour

HOUSE ON THE HILL—www.houseonthehill.net: cookie cutters, cookie molds

JOANN FABRIC AND CRAFT STORES—www.joann.com: craft paper, rubber stamps, cupcake papers and nonpareils.

KING ARTHUR FLOUR—www.kingarthurflour.com: espresso powder, cake flours

KITCHEN KRAFTS—www.kitchenkrafts.com: candy molds, bakeware

LORANN OILS—www.lorannoils.com: flavoring oils, specialty food colorings and candy making supplies; some LorAnn supplies available at Amazon.com

MCCORMICK—www.mccormick.com: spices and food colorings

MICHAEL'S—www.michaels.com: rubber stamps

PADERNO WORLD CUISINE—www.world-cuisine.com: makers of culinary equipment and purveyor of the *tuile* cookie spoon stencil

SUR LA TABLE—www.surlatable.com: mini-doughnut pan, large variety of baking pans and utensils

VALHRONA—www.valhrona.com: high-quality French chocolate; with its silky texture and deep chocolate flavor, this is the ultimate choice for all types of confections and baking.

WILLIAMS-SONOMA—www.williams-sonoma.com: petit fours molds, specialty spices and extracts, heavy-duty stand mixers

WILTON—www.wilton.com: fondant, piping tips, piping bags, fondant sculpture tools

ACKNOWLEDGMENTS

My eternal gratitude belongs to my literary agent, Lindsay Edgecombe, for this opportunity. Special thanks go to Nathaniel Marunas, who believed in this project and gave me the freedom to follow my muse wherever she led. I am also indebted to the talented crew at Sterling Publishing who helped bring this book to life: associate art director Christine Heun, designer Barbara Balch, line editor Wes Martin, editor Katherine Furman, managing editor Kimberly Marini, production manager Sal Destro, and photo editor Stacey Stambaugh.

Deep appreciation goes to artist and graphic designer Heather Ozee, who provided graphics for the Color chapter of this book; Morgan Trinker, for the photograph of me, Mark, and Biscuit in the introduction; and to Rebecca Schmidt Ruebensaal of Mr. Boddington's Studio, whose illustrations elevated this book to whole new level of cute.

A host of family and friends were of vital support. Thanks to my mother (prop master, recipe tester, dishwasher, and all-around partner in crime), who I hope I never have to do without; Pappy, for his council and Ecclesiastes 9:10; Ann Nelson, my dearest friend and the best artist I know; my husband Mark, for his technical genius; Megan Baird, the only other person who thinks it's a good idea to make 4 dozen sugar cookies after canning jelly all day; Carrie Bull, for "Merry Un-Birthday" inspiration; The Elders: Rosa Finley, Bessie Crutchfield, Ruby Ivey, Grace Crabtree, Katie Watts, Gail Baird, Lois Gibson, Pam Goans, and Linda Spitzer, whose food and love have sustained me, pastry chef Stella Parks, for recipe testing and advice; my first friend in all of blogdom, Sue Sparks, Dena Gray and my PathGroup family; pugs Biscuit and Churro, who sat on either side of me as I wrote this book in its entirety.

And, of course, more appreciation than I can express to the readers and supporters of *SprinkleBakes*.

INDEX

Note: Recipe titles followed by (*var.*) indicate recipe variations.